meet Me at the well
living water for thirsty teachers

by tracey kiesling

Copyright © 2007 by Tracey Kiesling

meet Me at the well
living water for thirsty teachers

written by Tracey Kiesling
cover design by Stacie Thompson

Printed in the United States of America

ISBN 978-1-60034-938-6
ISBN 1-60034-938-2
Library of Congress Number: TXu1-310-723

All rights reserved solely by the author. The author guarantees all contents are original and do not infringe upon the legal rights of any other person or work. No part of this book may be reproduced in any form without the permission of the author. The views expressed in this book are not necessarily those of the publisher.

Unless otherwise indicated, Bible quotations are taken from:
» The King James Version. Copyright © 1947 by A.J. Holman.
» Amplified. Copyright © 1965 by Zondervan.
» The Living Bible. Copyright © 1971 by Tyndale.
» New Living Translation. Copyright © 1996 by Tyndale.
» The Message. Copyright © 2002 by NavPress.
» Moffatt's. Copyright © 1954 by Kregel Publications.
» The Phillips Translation. Copyright © 1972 by Macmillan.

www.xulonpress.com

... but whoever drinks of the water that I shall give him shall never thirst; but the water that I shall give him shall become in him a well of water springing up to eternal life.

John 4:14

Dedication

This book is dedicated to the 1994-2001 staff of Brady High School, in Brady, Texas, in particular to Principal Preasly Cooper and Vice Principal Stan Seymour. We were all as close as any family could be. I love every one of these people, as they poured much into my life, and I cherish my fond memories of good times with all of them. My hope is that through this book I can give back into the lives of these special ones and offer encouragement to teachers everywhere.

I would also like to recognize the late Kenneth "Tootsie" Mitchell, superintendent of Rochelle, Texas ISD, who created a teaching position for me at a crucial time in my life.

Acknowledgements

I am so grateful to my daughter-in-law, Sara Thompson, a teacher herself, for her encouragement on this project. The few pages of this publication that I had written years ago were lying somewhere in a drawer, long forgotten. As Sara gained access to these and read them, she urged me to finish the work and publish it. Many words of encouragement also came from my stepdaughter-teacher, Katherine Pearce; her enthusiasm and zeal for teaching are unparalleled.

Credit for the magnificent cover goes to my talented and creative architect daughter-in-law, Stacie Thompson. I receive as love her endless hours of work to make this part of the book successful.

Others that I cannot leave out, as their prayers and support meant much to me during this time, are my mother Loais Williams; my sons, Trait and Ty Thompson; my son-in law Kevin Pearce; my dear friend and prayer partner, Mary Ann Wilson, and of course my dear husband, Donald Kiesling.

In addition, I am grateful to my faithful school prayer partner, Karen Andrews, and my friend Becky Martin, both English teachers who were essential to the editing process. Many thanks to Dr. Carl Baugh of Creation Evidence Museum, Glen Rose, Texas, for writing the foreword and for critique of the book.

I would also like to thank Elizabeth Ridenour and all who are connected with the National Council on Bible Curriculum in Public Schools.

Most of all, I am thankful to my Lord and Savior, Jesus Christ, for radically changing my life.

Foreword

Every school teacher in America should read this work by Tracey Kiesling. Author Kiesling demonstrates the mind of a teacher and the foresight of a philosopher. Throughout her teaching career she has exemplified the moral code and the spiritual concern that once made classroom teachers the most respected profession to the life of a student. By reading this book the teacher now becomes the student by catching the spirit of its author.

The teacher cannot teach the student to become what she is not. Tracey Kiesling is what she writes about, and every teacher can learn from her. The image and instruction of the teacher follow the student throughout life. More waking hours are spent before the teacher than before any other person, including parents. Genuine concern for every student and faculty member should guide fellow instructors "to be, rather than not to be." Author Kiesling shows you how.

Carl E. Baugh, Ph.D.
Founder, Creation Evidence Museum

Table of Contents

Day 1- The Calling of a Teacher 1
Day 2- The Value of a Prayer Partner 3
Day 3- Praying Over Your School 5
Day 4- Integrity and Character on the Job 7
Day 5- Remain in a State of Thankfulness 9
Day 6- His Grace for Your Tasks 11
Day 7- Let Me Tell You Why You're Here 13
Day 8- A Place for Your Heart 15
Day 9- Tough Love, Part One 17
Day 10- Tough Love, Part Two 19
Day 11- Stop Strife 21
Day 12- The Power of Holiness 23
Day 13- Be Teachable 25
Day 14- Be Steadfast 27
Day 15- Promises Kept 29
Day 16- Come Apart, Stay Together, Part One 31
Day 17- Come Apart, Stay Together, Part Two 33
Day 18- What You Need When You Need It 35
Day 19- God's Perfect Will 37
Day 20- Don't Leave Home Without Your Armor 39
Day 21- God's Magnificent Love 41
Day 22- Promotion 43
Day 23- Remain At Rest, Part One 45
Day 24- Remain At Rest, Part Two 47
Day 25- Set the Day 49
Day 26- Stay With the Glory 51
Day 27- The Power of Praise 53
Day 28- Best Laid Plans 55
Day 29- Real Self-Worth 57
Day 30- Not Number One 59
Day 31- Constructive Criticism 61
Day 32- Be Angry and Sin Not 63
Day 33- The Mouth 65
Day 34- Student Destiny, Part One 67
Day 35- Student Destiny, Part Two 69
Day 36- Joy Instead of Mourning 71
Day 37- Safe in the Secret Place 73
Day 38- Working Together 75
Day 39- High Expectations 77
Day 40- Go Ye 79
Day 41- Press Toward the Mark 81
Day 42- A Faithful Employee 83
Day 43- Idle Talk 85
Day 44- Radically Blessed 87

Day 45- Send Me? 89
Day 46- Stay Close, Go Far 91
Day 47- Man's Ways or God's Ways 93
Day 48- Factor in the Anointing 95
Day 49- Forever Settled 97
Day 50- The Power of One 99
Day 51- Pray the Word, Part One 101
Day 52- Pray the Word, Part Two 103
Day 53- The Wisdom of God 105
Day 54- Creativity, Part One 107
Day 55- Creativity, Part Two 109
Day 56- More Than Conquerors 111
Day 57- The Blessing of Friendship, Part One 113
Day 58- The Blessing of Friendship, Part Two 115
Day 59- To Come to the Rescue 117
Day 60- Consider Eternity 119
Day 61- Manifestations of the Holy Spirit 121
Day 62- Do Not Neglect Training 123
Day 63- Cast Your Care, Part One 125
Day 64- Cast Your Care, Part Two 127
Day 65- Knit Together 129
Day 66- Are You a Fruit-Bearer? Part One 131
Day 67- Are You a Fruit-Bearer? Part Two 133
Day 68- Are You a Fruit-Bearer? Part Three 135
Day 69- The Mercy of God, Part One 137
Day 70- The Mercy of God, Part Two 139
Day 71- From the Head, Part One 141
Day 72- From the Head, Part Two 143
Day 73- Diligence 145
Day 74- Covered and Protected, Part One 147
Day 75- Covered and Protected, Part Two 149
Day 76- The Sin of Pride 151
Day 77- A Different Look at Joy 153
Day 78- What's On You? 155
Day 79- Consequences of Complaining 157
Day 80- Another Kind of Teacher 159
Day 81- A Giving Mentality 161
Day 82- His Way is Always Success 163
Day 83- A Time of Cleansing 165
Day 84- The Final Outcome 167
Day 85- Two Job Descriptions 169
Day 86- My Favorite Teachers 171
Day 87- Training for Eternity 173
Day 88- By Faith 175
Day 89- Failure Sabotaged: My Story, Part One 177
Day 90- Failure Sabotaged: My Story, Part Two 179

The Calling of a Teacher

Day 1

Let not many of you become teachers, my brethren, that as such we shall incur a stricter judgment.
James 3:1, KJV

    I have often wondered why the above scripture does not describe lawyers, businessmen, doctors, or even preachers. It occurred to me that teachers must have the greatest opportunity to impress, change, or mold a person in a manner that would have lasting effects.
    Donna was a senior in one of my high school English classes many years ago. She was about to be married on the upcoming Saturday. As it happened, so was I. The Monday following our weddings, I came into class and before anything else took place, I made the announcement that since both Donna and I had new names, I would put them on the board so that everyone could start learning them. I did just that, writing them on the blackboard side by side. I was not particularly close to Donna, and after she graduated I did not see her again for several years. Then one night she and her husband, who now had two children, were invited to a Bible study that I was attending. When she saw me she came up and hugged me. Later the leaders of the Bible study told me that she had told them of the story of my writing our names side by side on the board and how important and confident it had made her feel about her new marriage. It took me by surprise! I had not even remembered the incident at first and had no idea at the time that I was doing something positive for a student.
    It was at that time I realized that my every move was being watched and noticed by someone in my classroom. It changed my whole perspective on teaching and being a teacher.

Pray this prayer: *Dear God: Thank you so much for the opportunity to serve you today in the capacity in which you have called me. I yield myself to the Holy Spirit in that what You want done will be done in this classroom. I am called and I am anointed and Your glory lives on the inside of me. Speak through me today and act through me today. In Jesus' name, Amen.*

The Value of a Prayer Partner

Day 2

Again I say unto you, That if two of you shall agree on earth as touching any thing that they shall ask, it shall be done for them of my Father which is in heaven.
Matthew 18:19, KJV

The first thing I did when I returned to teaching was find a prayer partner. God put me with a wonderful woman, Karen. We met regularly to pray, fast, and have Bible study. Others met with us through the years, but as they came and went, Karen remained faithful to the two of us putting everything else aside to pray for our school, faculty, and students. To this day we meet to agree in prayer over everything from the challenges in our nation to a particular student who may be having problems.

Praying in agreement is scriptural and in accordance with God's word. There is also great power in agreement. The Bible says that **"one can put a thousand to flight, and two ten thousand." (Deut. 32:30)**. Miracles are wrought through the prayers of two praying. Jesus said that where two or more are gathered, He is there in the midst of them.

In some cases there may be no one else praying about the things that affect your school. Ask God to show you today at least one person on staff to agree with you in prayer. He will answer you, and you will be amazed at the results of the prayers.

<u>Pray this prayer:</u> *Dear God, I believe you planted me here to make a difference. I believe that prayer works. I ask You today to put me together with at least one other praying person on this staff. Thank You for arranging the perfect time for us to pray in agreement together over the concerns of this school. In Jesus' name, Amen.*

meet Me at the well

Praying Over Your School

Day 3

...the earnest (heartfelt, continued) prayer of a righteous man makes tremendous power available--- dynamic in its working.

James 5:16, AMP

Schools, particularly public schools, are under tremendous attack by the enemy, Satan. The Bible says in Revelation 12:12 that the devil knows that he has only a short time left and so his strategy is to wreak havoc as much as possible. Young people are particularly susceptible and desperately need our prayers and support. Our school leaders are also under attack, particularly those who desire to expose our children to moral and Biblical principles.

Make a list of school- related things that need prayer coverage every day. Pray for superintendents, principals, faculty, students and janitorial staff. Pray for a spirit of repentance to fall and for the glory of God to flood the atmosphere. Enlist the prayer power of other interested parties, such as parents, grandparents, and other community members. Perhaps these would agree to walk the school grounds at different times of the day and pray.

I believe that our schools can be completely taken back and the forces of darkness abated. I believe that rebellion, addictions, lust, and apathy for learning can be defeated by the power of prayer and the blood of Jesus.

Today become determined to cry out to God in behalf of your school and expect the glory!

Pray this prayer: *Dear God, today I lift up this school. I bless this school. I thank You for the opportunity to serve you in this capacity. I plead the blood of Jesus over my superintendent (name), my principal (name), our faculty, students and janitorial staff. I pray that we soar on the wings of your grace. I draw the blood line* *around this school and I say that no weapon formed against it can prosper. With the blood and name of Jesus I come against the spirits of addiction, rebellion, lust, and apathy toward learning. I expect to see Your power and Your glory manifest in this school. In Jesus' name, Amen*

Integrity and Character on the Job

Day 4

I know that You are pleased with me, for my enemy does not triumph over me. In my integrity You uphold me and see me in Your presence forever.
Psalm 41:12, NIV

The Strong's Concordance references the word <u>**integrity**</u> as <u>completeness,</u> or, <u>complete truth.</u> Webster's Dictionary defines the same word as <u>perfect condition, soundness of sound moral principle, uprightness.</u>

On your job, what do you do when no one is looking? What do you do when no one is checking up on you? Are your principles always the same no matter what? Most people do a fair job when the boss or superior is close by, but many slack off when they think no one is looking.

Here are some specific things the Lord taught me about integrity on the job:

a. Walking down the halls, if there is trash on the floor, pick it up. (Is this my job? No. Will anyone appreciate it or thank me? Probably not. DO IT ANYWAY).
b. Turn off lights and keep the temperature in moderate ranges.
c. Do not "borrow" items that belong to the school, such as classroom equipment, paper clips, rubber bands, paper, etc.
d. Do not attend to personal business on the school's time, unless given special permission.

There are many other situations that I have not listed. Let the Holy Spirit lead you in this. Remember, God will uphold you in your integrity and set you in his presence forever. WOW! Develop an attitude of integrity today.

Prayer this prayer: *Dear God, I ask you today to show me the places in my life where I may not be operating in integrity. I know it must grieve You when your people act like the world and are slack in integrity. I ask You to change my heart. By the power of the Holy Spirit I determine to walk in integrity whether anyone is looking or not. Thank You, that You uphold me in my integrity and set me in Your presence forever. In Jesus' name, Amen.*

Remain in a State of Thankfulness

Day 5
That I may publish with the voice of thanksgiving...
Psalm 26:7, KJV

Neither murmur ye, as some of them also murmured, and were destroyed of the destroyer...
1 Corinthians 10:10, KJV

Nothing moves the heart of God as much as an attitude of thankfulness. I once heard a minister that I highly respect tell this story. He and one of his friends went night hunting. They had a taped recording of sounds that were similar to those of a hurt or wounded animal. The sounds resembled those of moaning, groaning, and complaining. Within only moments of beginning play of the tape, predators began coming up to the site where they were hiding and watching. The minister said that immediately the Lord showed him what happens when **WE** moan, groan, or complain. IT IMMEDIATELY DRAWS THE ENEMY!

Do you walk around your halls, offices, and classrooms in an attitude of thankfulness no matter what? Or are you always complaining? Have you truly stopped to think about all you have to be thankful for? One of my colleagues was a man who is paralyzed and in a wheelchair. He puts out more effort just **getting to school** every morning than most people put out all day long. Every time I look at him I am so grateful that my body is healthy and well.

From the time you awaken, begin to praise and thank the Lord; then look for things all day long for which to be thankful. Do not fall into the trap of moaning, groaning, and complaining. It shuts the ears of God and draws the enemy.

<u>Pray this prayer:</u> *Dear God, forgive me when I complain or have a bad attitude. Help me to change my focus from the negative to the* *positive. Today, Lord, I enter Your gates with thanksgiving and Your courts with praise. I refuse to fall into the trap of moaning, groaning, and complaining. Holy Spirit, quicken me immediately and reveal to me if I even begin to complain. In the name of Jesus, Amen.*

His Grace For Your Tasks

Day 6

...If only I may finish the race and complete the task the Lord Jesus has given me—the task of testifying to the gospel of God's grace.

Acts 20:24, NIV

The word of **grace** in this scripture carries the meaning, acceptable benefit, favor, or gift in the Strong's Concordance. I could never have accomplished anything in the classroom without God's grace on me. There were so many times that I thought I just could not make it through the day, and then "somehow", by the time 3:30 came, I had eased through it.

Even the most seasoned teacher cannot do the same thing every year in the classroom, because there is a different group of students who require a different game plan. There were a few years that I fell very short of my goals as a teacher because I tried to implement the exact same plan over and over each school year. Finally, with the help and guidance of the Holy Spirit, I discovered that only through God's grace and leading could I ever hope to reach each individual set of students.

There is a song with this line: "I need your grace to cover me, come in like a flood and carry me under, flow like a river over me…" Flow in the grace of God today and realize your full potential to finish the race and complete the task the Lord Jesus has given you. He is waiting to pour out His "undeserved favor, benefit, and gift" on you today.

Pray this prayer: *Dear God, I acknowledge that I need to flow in Your grace today to successfully reach my students. I thank You that because of the blood shed at Calvary, and because I am Your* *child, I have access to that grace. By faith, I receive Your grace now and I thank You for it. In Jesus' name, Amen.*

Let Me Tell You Why You're Here

Day 7

Let me tell you why you are here. You're here to be salt-seasoning that brings out the God-flavors of the earth....Here's another way to put it: You're here to be light, bringing out the God-colors in the world. God is not a secret to be kept...Keep open house, be generous with your lives. By opening up to others, you'll prompt people to open up with God...

Matthew 5:13,14, The Message

Do you want to witness to others? Then here is your highest calling: **live the Christian life wherever God has planted you.** "Is that it?" you may be saying. What about reaching the lost in Africa? What about preaching to millions? What about street ministry, pulpit ministry, prison ministry? Thank God for all those callings. But there are so many lost and hurting people in the world who have seen Christian people NOT LIVING the victorious Christian life. These people have decided that Christianity is just a show, not anything any different than the way they themselves live.

Right in your classroom there are students who are crying out for role models who don't talk one way and live another. Right in the classroom next door there is a teacher who has no joy. In the office downstairs may be a secretary or an administrator who desperately needs a word of encouragement. Up and down the hallways walk students who need a warm smile or hug.

Here are some ways to live the victorious Christian life on a daily basis in the workplace:

1. Exhibit joy in your life. Don't walk in the door on Monday morning grumbling about how far away Friday is. Keep a song on your lips.
2. Always be readily available with these words on your lips: How may I help you?

3. Do not spend too much time in the teacher's lounge socializing. Avoid gossiping and negative talk.
4. Come to work early and be willing to stay late.
5. Treat everyone with great importance, from janitor to superintendent.

Pray this prayer: *Dear God, thank You for helping me today to be Your greatest possible witness by living Your Word. I may be the only Jesus people see today, so by the power of Your Holy Spirit, I let Your light shine through me and be salt seasoning. In Jesus' name, Amen.*

A Place For Your Heart

Day 8

Know the state of your flocks, and put your heart into caring for your herds...
Proverbs 27:23, New Living

Although working in a school offers many opportunities for helping those around you, at the heart of your responsibilities are the students.

I always made a point of quickly learning my students' names or what they preferred to be called. By the second or third day of school I knew at least all of their first names. I also made it a point to learn any other information I could about them that would be helpful in getting to know them as a person, not just a member of a class. Also, before each day began, I walked my classroom praying scriptures for my classes as a whole. Many times the Holy Spirit would bring particular students to mind for prayer. Often I sat in each individual desk and prayed by name for the students that sat there all day long. This generally took days to do, but it is well worth the time for these reasons:

    a. Some students have absolutely no one praying for them.
    b. I believe prayer helps their particular situations.
    c. It helped me to see even the most difficult students through the eyes of love and compassion.
    d. Prayer in my classroom on a continual basis helped maintain peace.

Do you know the state of your flocks? I urge you today to get quiet before the Lord and ask Him how you can become more personally involved with your students. It may save a life.

Pray this prayer: *Dear God, Your word says to know the state of my flocks. I want my students to know that not only do I care for* *them, but that You care for them as well. Even though it may look as though my time is already stretched, would You supernaturally increase my time and show me ways to reach out to my students. Show me what to pray over them. Help me to show them love. In Jesus' name, Amen.*

Tough Love, Part One

Day 9

He opens their ear to instruction and discipline...
Job 36:10, AMP

I find it interesting that this scripture combines the words **instruction** and **discipline.** Without discipline there will be little instruction in the classroom. Also, students want and need discipline.

One of the most difficult things a new teacher struggles with is finding the balance between discipline and camaraderie in the classroom. At the beginning of each new school year I made this announcement to my students: "I am under contract to teach you. You are under contract to learn. These are our respective jobs. I would really like to be your friend, but if it comes down to being your friend or doing my job, I will choose my job. If we both do our jobs conscientiously, friendship will automatically occur."

The next thing I would do is set down rules so that the students will know exactly where they stand. But remember, these rules are of no benefit unless enforced. For example, my students were tardy if they were not seated at the moment the tardy bell **began** to ring. This may seem a little harsh, but it makes it black and white for them. Also, since classroom time is so short, instruction needs to begin as soon as possible. For the first few days some of the students tried me; but as soon as they saw that I enforced the rule, I not only had few to no tardies the rest of the year, but class started immediately after the last bell. Enforced rules are also helpful in another way: I never had to raise my voice in the classroom, yet discipline remained tantamount. By the end of the day I had also kept my joy! Ultimately, the balance of discipline and camaraderie occurred.

<u>Pray this prayer:</u> *Dear God, give me the strength to discipline my class so that proper instruction may take place. Open my eyes to* *ways of discipline that work with my particular students. Open my students' ears and hearts to instruction and discipline. Today I will listen for the voice of the Holy Spirit to lead me in manners and methods in my classroom. In Jesus' name, Amen.*

Tough Love, Part Two

Day 10

...but what do your arguments prove?

Job 6:25b, NIV

Having taught and having been involved with public school for over twenty years, as well as having reared four children of my own, I have discovered that children are masters at drawing adults into an argument. The object is control, or, getting you to change your mind to their way of thinking.

Arguing is very detrimental to the discipline of the classroom. First, it wastes valuable class time. Second, it may give way to anger. Third, the teacher loses some amount of respect because ground is lost and rules are compromised.

It is interesting to note that Eve got into an argumentative conversation with the devil in Gen. 3:1-6. He was able to plant doubt into her mind, and as a result, she and Adam disobeyed God and began the process of death for us all.

If a student begins to question a rule, or why you did this or that, or accuses you of treating another student one way and him/her another, be on the lookout for an impending argument. Refuse to be drawn into the argument. Instead, simply state how things are going to be and then speak no more. If necessary, turn your back or leave the room if possible. Immediately continue on with the lesson or project at hand to change the subject and atmosphere.

NOTE: Be sensitive to the isolated times when an explanation is warranted. Remember that in a confrontation it is always wise to stop and get quiet for a moment and allow the Holy Spirit to guide you in the situation. His way will always work!

<u>Pray this prayer:</u> *Dear God, thank You for helping me to be sensitive to the Holy Spirit's guidance today. Thank You for helping me flow with wisdom and tact in each situation. Help me to keep my words soft and kind. I refuse to argue, or to be drawn into* *an argument. Help me to settle all issues in a peaceful manner. In Jesus' name, Amen.*

Stop Strife

Day 11

The beginning of strife is as when water first trickles; therefore, stop contention before it becomes worse and quarreling breaks out.
Proverbs 17:14, AMP

For where envying and strife is, there is confusion and every evil work.
James 3:16, KJV

It seems that there is so much strife in the workplace, and particularly in a school setting. The arts department is upset because the athletic department received more new equipment. This teacher is upset because that teacher was chosen for a particular honor. This teacher has to sponsor three events or clubs and that teacher only has to sponsor one. The list goes on.

The root of strife, of course, comes from the enemy, Satan. And the main goal is to stop the work of God. If God has called you to the teaching/school position, then there is great destiny and purpose for you in that place. There is a very important job for you to do there. When you get a revelation of this picture of destiny in Him, your focus should never be on anything else.

Refuse to be a part of any strife-producing situations or talk that goes on in your school. Be a peacemaker whenever possible. Do not become offended if someone else is chosen over you. Notice in the Bible that Jesus NEVER became offended. He is our example. If a problem arises between you and a co-worker, go to him/her and be honest and open about discussing it. Be quick to forgive and ask for forgiveness. Never lose sight of the reason that you are in that work place.

Pray this prayer: *Dear God, thank You for calling me to a great plan and purpose in this school. By faith, I place a protective hedge around myself and my ears that blocks out strife-producing talk and situations. I refuse to be a cause or a part of envying or strife. Help me always to be a peacemaker, for you have said in Your word that they shall be called children of God. In Jesus' name, Amen.*

The Power of Holiness

Day 12

But as the One Who called you is holy, you yourselves also be holy in all your conduct and manner of living.

1 Peter 1:15, AMP

Worship the Lord with the beauty of holy lives.
Psalm 96:9, TLB

Holiness is basic to walking in the power of God. Holiness is not necessarily just reading your Bible every day, praying every day, or being in church every time the doors are open, although these are all good things to do.

One essential part of holiness is allowing God to sanctify us or set us apart. Jesus said, **"Sanctify them—purify, consecrate, separate them for Yourself, make them holy—by the Truth. Your word is Truth." (John 17:17)**

So how do we walk in the holiness that He commanded us? By staying in the Word and allowing it to change and mold our thoughts, attitudes, and actions. Romans 6:21, 22 says, **"What benefit did you reap at that time from the things you are now ashamed of? Those things result in death! But now that you have been set free from sin and have become slaves to God, the benefit you reap leads to holiness, and the result is eternal life."** I remember years ago when I began allowing the truth of the Word to change my life. I totally lost the desire to watch certain things, listen to certain things, wear certain clothing, and go certain places for entertainment. I do not miss those things at all. The benefits of laying those things down have been huge, and the richness of my life has dramatically increased.

What does all of this have to do with being a teacher? Teaching in the 21st century is more challenging than ever before. A teacher may be the only positive role model some students see. As a teacher, one needs to access ALL the power of God in order to be successful. Holiness is at the very core. Get into the Word today and allow the Truth to sanctify and make you holy. You will walk as a powerful witness to those around you.

Pray this prayer: *Dear God, I choose to walk holy as You are holy. I invite You to shine Your light into areas of my heart that now fall short of true holiness. Help me to make the adjustments necessary to walk a holy and just life. I desire to please You, Father, by walking holy and upright. I desire a closer union with Jesus. Change my heart so that His desires are my desires, and may the fruit be visible in my outward life. In Jesus' name, Amen.*

Be Teachable

Day 13

Strategic planning is the key to warfare; to win you need a lot of good counsel.

Proverbs 24:6, The Message

It is very important, particularly as a new teacher, that you take advantage of all the counsel and experience available to you. Veteran teachers have many ideas of what works and what does not work in many given situations. Ideas about teaching, discipline, making lesson plans, making bulletin boards, and handling various student challenges are available from others all around you.

Do not be too proud to ask more experienced teachers for ideas. This does not mean that you have to implement all those ideas. Ask your principal for permission to sit in on the classes of other teachers. Take notes and then ask the teacher questions afterward about certain procedures, lessons, etc. Find out about staff development workshops or conferences in your subject matter area and attend those.

As each teaching year passes, you will combine your ideas with the ideas of others to form your own patterns. Although my primary teaching field is Spanish, I also taught a Bible History class at our public school. One of the requirements was to memorize scripture verses. Some of the students complained that memorizing was too hard and that it just could not be done. Knowing how important memorization in general is, I wanted to prove a point. One day I had an idea, and I took their challenge to memorize the 119th Psalm (176 verses!) and quoted it for them. They never again complained about memorizing.

Pray this prayer: *Dear God, help me to remain teachable. Help me to be alert to new ideas that may be used in my classroom. Help me to be sensitive to times when I need counsel. Holy Spirit, you are* *the "**Counselor, Helper, Advocate, Intercessor, Strengthener (John 14:16)** and I depend on you first of all. In Jesus' name, Amen.*

Be Steadfast

Day 14

Those who trust in the Lord are steady as Mount Zion, unmoved by any circumstance.

Psalm 125 1 TLB

Do your circumstances determine the tone of your day? One of the greatest witnesses to others around you is your conduct in the midst of your circumstances.

I remember one August in particular. One week into the school year, my sister, who also worked at the same school as a school nurse, had to have emergency surgery for a life-threatening condition. She clinically died twice on the operating table. In the middle of this ordeal, my father had a heart attack in a city several miles the other direction. To complicate matters further, I had the largest classes and the most students I had ever had. There were not even enough desks in the room for all of them! In the natural, all of this would be overwhelming. I remember turning to the Word and prayer during this time. As I walked the halls that week, or spent the night with my sister in ICU, I would sing praises to the Lord, remembering His faithfulness.

My classes continued to run smoothly, my sister received a series or miracle healings, and my father is alive and well today. I remember a sense of "peace that passes all understanding" flooding over me. Later, I overheard others around me saying they did not know why I was not falling apart. The answer is easy: trust in the Lord, believe His word, and do not be moved by circumstances.

Pray this prayer: *Dear God, help me keep my eyes fixed on You and not fall prey to my circumstances. I recognize You as my Rock. By the power of the Holy Spirit, help me to remember that as I pray and believe Your word, I don't have to live "under the circumstances." I refuse to allow situations from the devil to* *control my reactions and behavior, for You are bigger than any of these. In Jesus' name, Amen.*

Promises Kept

Day 15
>*And so after waiting patiently, Abraham received what was promised.*
>
>   *Hebrews 6:15, NIV*

God promised Abraham a son of his own, a son with his wife Sarah. But it was many years afterward that Abraham received that promise.

Many times in my teaching career I was tempted with the thought that nothing I was doing was making any difference. I would often have to remind myself of the prayer my younger sister prayed over me when I returned to the teaching field. She prayed that I would not be moved or influenced by failure to see instant results. It may be many years down the road before we as teachers realize how greatly we impacted our students. Since this is the case, we must simply be glad to be a servant of the Lord in this capacity. We have to trust that **something** we are doing is making a difference.

It is helpful to keep this perspective because then we can give God the glory every day for what he is accomplishing through each one of us. I learned that I do not need to be thanked or recognized every day. All that is necessary is to know that God working through me made a difference in a child's life. So the next time the devil tries to convince you that nothing you are doing matters, take that as a sure sign that what you are doing matters greatly indeed!

<u>Pray this prayer:</u> Dear God, thank You for working through me today. I determine now that whether or not I see results will not matter. Lead me to make a difference in the life of every child with

whom I come in contact today. Give me the confidence to know that I made deposits in a child's life today. In Jesus' name, Amen.

Come Apart, Stay Together
Part One

Day 16

And when he had sent the multitudes away, he went into a mountain apart to pray; and when evening was come, he was there alone.
Matthew 14:23, KJV

How well does your day stay together? The secret to a "stay together" day is to come apart and get before Him every single day before you do anything else. We see in the Scriptures how often Jesus went off alone to pray. That must mean that getting alone with the Father is a very integral part of the day. There are so many things that God will speak to us as we get alone with Him in the early, quiet part of the day. Oh, how many catastrophes might be avoided by giving the Father the first part of the day? We see Jesus often go up on a mountain or out into a garden to pray. Sometimes he prayed all night long.

Many times, as I have arisen early to pray before going to school, I have received exactly what plan I needed for each period of the day. Sometimes it would be an answer concerning how to handle a situation with a particular student.

I believe the purpose of the three-year ministry of Jesus on the earth was at least, in part, to teach us how to live the victorious life. It was so simple, yet even the disciples missed it. Jesus made a habit of consulting the Father on a regular basis. If Jesus did this, certainly we must as well!

<u>Pray this prayer:</u> *Dear God, I want to follow the pattern of Jesus and spend time alone with You every single day. I start right now, today, to form the habit of consulting You on a regular basis. Thank You, that in this quiet time together, You will show me many* *things I need to know for a "stay together" day. In Jesus' name, Amen.*

Come Apart, Stay Together
Part Two

Day 17
> *I am distracted by the noise of the enemy…*
> *Psalm 55:3, AMP*

Your enemy Satan will try very hard to keep you from getting alone on a regular basis in the presence of the Lord. This is because he knows that prayer, fellowship with Jesus, and reading the Bible will completely change your life and cause you to walk in victory.

The number one excuse for not having a quiet time is lack of time. Martin Luther said: "I am so busy that I cannot afford **not** to pray at least four hours every day." **Four hours?!** Yes, and that was back in the days when we didn't chase children to numerous activities, race on the freeway to work, and attend several social events during the week. So even then the enemy used lack of time as an excuse.

Most people have no trouble scheduling in what is really important to them. We have no trouble scheduling golf games, hair and nail appointments, parties, and outings with friends. There is nothing wrong with any of these things. But are they taking you to a higher level? Are they improving the quality of your life?

Determine now to "schedule in" God. That may sound insensitive, but after only a few days of being in the presence of God, it will become your heart's burning desire to be in quiet times of fellowship with Him. You will fight for time and put everything else aside to get into His presence. Here are some suggestions for arranging your time: get up half an hour earlier; turn off the television, or take your Bible to school and spend your lunch hour with Him. When you do this, everyone around you is affected as well!

<u>Pray this prayer:</u> *Dear God, help me reschedule my priorities. I really want to have a quiet time with You. Right now I determine* *not to listen to the excuses that the enemy whispers in my ear. Reveal Yourself to me in our quiet times together. I listen to You each day for my marching orders. In Jesus' name, Amen*

What You Need When You Need It

Day 18

For the Holy Spirit will teach you what needs to be said even as you are standing there.
Luke 12:12, New Living

Have you ever been teaching your class, knowing that the students were not grasping a particular concept? Or have you ever decided as the students were walking into class that you needed to do something different than what you originally had planned for the day? In these situations you do not have much time to get creative action moving because students get restless and focus is lost quickly.

In these times I have learned to stop briefly for a few seconds and pray in the Holy Ghost quietly under my breath. I may walk around the room for a moment using a distraction of some sort for the children while I wait to hear from the Holy Spirit. He has never failed to give me a great idea! More often than not it was an idea that far surpassed the original plan that I had. I knew only the Lord could have done that.

Use your greatest resource, the Holy Spirit, when teaching your classes. He knows much more than you do! He will show you the perfect lesson plan every time.

Pray this prayer: *Dear God, thank You so much for providing us with the Holy Spirit. Today I will listen for what You tell me through the person of the Holy Spirit. Give me listening ears and a hearing heart so that I might know Your perfect plan for my classes today. In Jesus' name, Amen.*

meet Me at the well

God's Perfect Will

Day 19

Paul, an apostle (special messenger) of Christ Jesus, the Messiah, by divine will—the purpose and the choice of God...

Ephesians 1:1, AMP

Do not be senseless, but understand what is the Lord's will.

Ephesians 5:17, Moffatt's

Are you in God's perfect will or His permissive will? Are you called to be a teacher?
I do not ask these questions to create doubt in your mind. Once, one of my students was staying after school making up missed work. Quite unexpectedly, she asked me a question, "Mrs. Kiesling, why do so many teachers act depressed and unhappy?" Although the question caught me off guard somewhat, I knew she was right and I wanted to answer her correctly. I paused for a time and then finally said, "I suppose it is because they desire to do something else."
Your job should not be just "a job". It should be a calling. Do you arrive early, excited about starting the day and projects with students? Do you stay late, desiring to complete some idea or project for the next day or week? Are you as joyful on Monday as on Friday? Do you miss your classroom or school atmosphere during vacations? Are you always getting new ideas even when school is not in session? If you can answer "yes" to most of these questions, more than likely you are called to be in the teaching field and are in God's perfect will.
Being in God's perfect will is much more exciting than being in His permissive will. It is also the safest place to be. The safest place on earth could be the most dangerous out of the will of God. And, the most dangerous place on earth could be the safest in the perfect will of God. Search your heart today and spend time alone with Him. If you are less than excited

about your job, perhaps it is time to pray about other options. Something has been finished since before the foundation of the world that YOU were born to begin.

Pray this prayer: Dear God, I want to be in Your perfect will. I want to work at a calling, not just go to a job every day. Shine light in my heart and mind as I examine those areas today. I yield to You and am willing to follow Your divine destiny for my life. In Jesus' name, Amen.

Don't Leave Home Without Your Armor

Day 20
Put on the whole armor of God, that ye may be able to stand against the wiles of the devil.
Ephesians 6:11, KJV

If you are a born again, blood bought believer, you have access to the armor of God. (If you don't know Jesus as your Savior and do not have a personal relationship with Him, stop now and pray this prayer: **"Dear God, I am a sinner. But I do not want to sin any more and serve the kingdom of darkness. Jesus, come into my heart and make it your home. I believe that you died on the cross and rose from the dead. Forgive me of my sins. Live now through me. I receive you as my Lord and Savior now.")**

We live in the most dangerous times ever. In the past several years we have even seen violence in the public schools, a place many thought would always be safe. When you think about it, there is actually no safe place. So put on your armor every day. Read Ephesians 6:10-18 to find out more about the armor of God.

When you put on the armor, the devil will not recognize you. He will think that is Jesus he's dealing with. You are protected on every side. How do you put on the armor? By releasing words of faith. Every single morning, the first thing you should do is put on the armor. Go step by step through Ephesians 6:10-17 and apply it to yourself. Do not even be concerned if you do not understand it all—do it by faith and God will teach you about it all. Pray the prayer below to put on the armor and do not leave home without it.

<u>Pray this prayer:</u> *Dear God, thank You for providing me with Your armor. Today I put on the whole armor of God. I put truth on my loins. I put on the breastplate of righteousness; my feet are shod with the preparation of the gospel of peace. I take the shield of faith so that I can quench every fiery dart of the wicked one. I put* on the helmet of salvation, and I'll not leave home without the sword of the Spirit, which is the word of God. In Jesus' name, Amen.

God's Magnificent Love

Day 21

Yet the Lord longs to be gracious to you; he rises to show compassion.

Isaiah 30:18, NIV

And we have known and believed the love God hath to us...

1 John 4:16, KJV

When you get the revelation that God loves you so much that He longs to show Himself to you, everything you do and think will change. The classroom is just one of the places He cares about in your life.

He wants to make every step you make. He wants to show you every direction to go. He wants to just be with you, to wrap His arms around you every day and be your "daddy". I grew up without a father in the home and it took a while for me to realize just how much God wants to be my Father. Not only can I come to Him for all needs and wants, but more important, I can tell Him I just want to sit down and talk a while. I just want to share my heart and my mind and my hurts.

Sometimes we get "religious" about God. We think that if we are not praying about the hungry in India, or the situations in the Middle East, or the sick and suffering that God will not listen to us. I enjoy playing tennis. One day I was on the way to the tennis court. I had not been playing well the last couple of weeks. I really wanted to play better that evening just to have a little more fun. Suddenly on the inside of me I heard the Holy Spirit say, "Why don't you pray about it?" My initial reaction was that God would never listen to such a trivial prayer. But immediately I remembered His great love for me, and that whatever is important to me is important to Him. I said a quick prayer and just thanked God for victory. I played much better that evening and had a great time. Did my overall tennis improve? Probably not. That would take just plain practice and instruction. The point is God showed me that He loves me **so** much that He even cared about a trivial game of tennis.

Pray this prayer: *Dear God, I thank You for loving me so much. I know that You did marvelous things for me, like sending Your son Jesus to the cross to die for me. But help me also to never forget to include You in what may even seem like the trivial things of life. I know that You long to be a part of everything I do. I love You and worship You. In Jesus' name, Amen.*

Promotion

Day 22

Do you see a man diligent and skillful in his business? He will stand before kings; he will not stand before obscure men.

Proverbs 22:29, AMP

Do you desire a promotion? Begin to talk to the Lord about it.

In the state where I was teaching school, it **appeared** that no one could really get a promotion. Teachers of the same years' experience would receive the same salaries regardless of whether or not they were good teachers. So even if an administrator believed a particular teacher to be the best, there was no such thing as simply getting a raise and a promotion.

Even so, I had been praying and studying the Bible concerning promotion. One year, my principal approached me about teaching a long distance class for another school that had no Spanish teacher. This was done through short circuit television. It was no extra work, except for having a few more students; I would be teaching the class at the same time as one of my other regular classes. I agreed to do it, and it gave me another paycheck. Also, I was able to meet and enjoy the students in person as they traveled to our school right before Christmas to participate in a project with our class. I saw this whole situation as a promotion in a place where there is none in the natural.

God can promote you no matter where you are. Joseph in the book of Genesis is a very good example. He was promoted right out of prison to second in command in Egypt! But notice the first part of the verse above: "...a man diligent and skillful in his business." Cultivate those things and then pray and expect promotion.

Pray this prayer: *Dear God, I know that You are the Promoter. First I ask You to show me ways to develop diligence and skill in my teaching. Father, I ask You to promote me. I ask that my work habits and ethics would be a witness to those around me. I thank You for promotion and I give You all the glory. In Jesus' name, Amen.*

Remain At Rest, Part One

Day 23

The Lord will fight for you, and you shall hold your peace and remain at rest.

Exodus 14:14, AMP

During the school year it seems that the spring semester is always full of activities. There are all kinds of spring sports, literary competitions, state testing, spring assemblies, and field trips. I remember sometimes feeling overwhelmed, because even without interruptions it is a real challenge for a teacher to cover all the necessary material.

One particular day I had several students missing in several different classes, and then one class period was used for an assembly. My initial feeling was of frustration as I once again altered the carefully prepared lesson plans. Then down deep in my spirit, with my "spiritual ears" I heard this: "Just rest." You see, there are all kinds of "setups" from the enemy to get you upset. If he can just get you out of peace and joy, then **nothing** will be accomplished.

I stopped for a few moments, took a deep breath and became quiet. Then I prayed and asked God to restore and even multiply the lost time in some way, shape, or form so that I could cover the necessary material without stress or fuss. By the end of the school year, I found it was all done, and I even covered some unplanned material. God is so faithful.

Pray this prayer: *Dear God, thank You that You fight for me so that I can rest. Help me to always remember that. I determine to rest in Your peace and know that everything is proceeding right on schedule. I release my faith now and trust in You. In Jesus' name, Amen.*

meet Me at the well

Remain At Rest, Part Two

Day 24

It is senseless to work so hard from early morning until late at night, fearing you will starve to death; for God wants His loved ones to get their proper rest.
                              Psalm 127:2, TLB

Recent research indicates that proper amounts of **rest** and sleep are essential to a healthy, productive immune system. A healthy immune system fights off disease and **keeps** our bodies sound. To function at peak in the classroom, **one** must be healthy.

Most of us make demands on our bodies without putting in deposits. I know from my own experiences that I **put** too much wear and tear on my body without always considering the consequences. The Scriptures make it clear why we do this. It boils down to fear of not being able to produce enough.

Begin today to make a habit of going to bed and getting up at the same time every day. Learn to draw a line where work ought to begin and end. In the afternoons or evenings after school, do something that you consider relaxing: take a walk, play a round of golf, work on a hobby that you enjoy. If at all possible, take a short nap every day. I know, I know! You are probably like I am: **a nap?? Who would have time for that?** But studies show that a "power nap" of fifteen or twenty minutes increases our energy to make it through the rest of the evening.

The bottom line is to trust God. He did not intend for us to work sixteen hours a day, or have two or three jobs. Trust Him today and get some rest.

<u>Pray this prayer:</u> *Dear God, I know that rest is a very important part of being healthy. In order to do all You have called me to do, I need to be healthy. Help me to gauge my days and to get plenty of* rest. I trust You to provide everything I need. I know that I cannot do it in my own strength. Thank You for being my strength today and helping me to get everything done. In Jesus' name, Amen.

Set The Day

Day 25

The light in the eyes of him whose heart is joyful rejoices the heart of others, and good news nourishes the bones.

Proverbs 15:30, AMP

Every morning I watched my first period class drag in sleepily. They seemed particularly sluggish on Monday mornings. Sometimes I felt the same way myself.

One day it dawned on me that I could set the tone of the entire day for these students. I decided to change the atmosphere in that first period class. I started playing music on my CD player. I played instrumental or classical music. As the bell rang and they walked into the room, they would immediately notice the music. Of course, I also greeted them at the door with a smile and positive words. Whenever possible I would begin class with something upbeat, such as a game or an oral exercise. I always smiled a lot and displayed a lot of energy. Sometimes I just talked with all of them for a few moments about their weekend or an upcoming school event.

There were some mornings that I did not really **feel** like doing any of these things. But I found that if I ignored my feelings and did them anyway, even I had a much better day! Brighten the lives of your students today and you will be brighter too.

Pray this prayer: *Dear God, thank You that I can be a carrier of good news. Help me brighten the day of my students by allowing Your light to shine through me in various and creative ways. Help me to set a tone for their day that carries even into their evenings at* home. Let me never forget how important this might be to just one individual. In Jesus' name, Amen.

Stay With The Glory

Day 26

Thus they exchanged Him Who was their glory for the image of an ox that eats grass—they traded their honor for the image of a calf! They forgot their Savior...
Psalm 106:20, 21a, AMP

The glory of God is discussed all throughout the Bible. Interestingly enough, one of the most common meanings of the word <u>**glory**</u> is <u>weight</u> or <u>weightiness.</u> God is a heavyweight! Can you imagine exchanging your heavyweight for a calf? God, who had fought all the Israelites' battles, and had delivered them out of bondage, and had carried them over the Red Sea and through the desert by His glory, was exchanged for an ox.

What kinds of exchanges do we make today? We exchange prayer time in the morning for another hour of sleep. We exchange Bible reading time in the evening for a couple of hours of television. We might even exchange Sunday morning church for a hobby or other activity. It might be important to read on in the Bible and find out what happened to the Israelites as a result of exchanging the glory and forgetting their Savior.

Being a success in the classroom partially depends on having the right answers at the right times. Since before the foundation of the world, God knew you were going to be in a classroom at this particular time in history. He has already provided for every single answer you need, but you have to do the work of tapping into His resources and putting His answers into practice.

Rest and fun do have a place in our lives. However, if you are exchanging the things of God for the things of the world on a regular basis, you are not living in the glory. Remember that in the glory is power. Keep growing in the things of God and stay in the glory.

Pray this prayer: *Dear God, I want to live in the glory. Help me to desire the things of You more and the things of this world less. I determine now not to exchange the glory for the things of this world. I will walk by the Spirit and stay in the glory. Thank You for being my "heavyweight." In Jesus' name, Amen.*

The Power of Praise

Day 27

Oh, that men would praise and confess to the Lord His goodness and loving kindness, and His wonderful works to the children of men!
Psalm 107:8,15,21,31, AMP

In Psalm 107, this scripture is repeated four times! After each, the mighty works of God are emphasized. Here are some of the works of His hand:

1. **He satisfies the longing soul and fills the hungry soul**
2. **He breaks apart bonds**
3. **He breaks gates of bronze**
4. **He sends His word and heals**
5. **He hushes storms to a calm**
6. **He turns wildernesses into pools of water**
7. **He raises the poor and needy from affliction**

Has God ever done any of these things for you? He has done them for me over and over again. Teaching high school students regularly lent itself to moments of frustration. I found the power of praise to be like no other. Praise would take my mind off the problems and put it on The Answer: Jesus. Plus, I would just feel better. Verse 43 of this Psalm says: **"Whoso is wise will observe and heed these things, and they will diligently consider the mercy and loving kindness of the Lord."**

Today take a look at everything He has done for you and then begin to praise Him. Praise Him for the things He is doing now, even if you do not see the results of them yet. Tell of His works to everyone you see.

<u>Pray this prayer:</u> *Dear God, I praise and thank You for the marvelous ways You have worked in my life. Remind me of them often, that I may share them with others. Never let me forget that* *even now You are working on things that concern me. In Jesus' name, Amen.*

Best Laid Plans

Day 28
Commit to the Lord whatever you do and your plans will succeed.
Proverbs 16:3, NIV

Most people have heard the phrase, "Best laid plans of mice and men…" This often means that all hard work and planning ended up as naught. This will never happen if we commit our plans to Him.

Most teachers think of lesson plans whenever the word **plans** is mentioned. Very few times have I written lesson plans that did not change almost immediately. Perhaps the week was interrupted by an unexpected assembly. Perhaps the weather turned inclement and a day of school was missed. Maybe I simply did not get as far as I thought I would in a particular lesson. All of these interruptions to lesson plans are minor when compared to those in the plans of life.

Each day when you arise, it is vital that you spend quiet time just listening to the voice of the Lord. Make certain you are hearing correctly by judging everything by His word. Verbally commit your plans to Him to do as He pleases in your life. Listen for your "marching orders" for the day. Be ready and sensitive to unexpected changes. EXPECT to be a blessing to all with whom you come into contact. There may be times when God will call on you to alter your plan right in the middle of a project or day. Even a slight adjustment may mean the difference in failure and success. When you make it a habit of doing this each day, know that whatever you do will succeed.

Pray this prayer: *Dear God, I listen for Your voice today. I commit every plan that I have to You. I make Your plans my plans. I fully* *expect to walk in success today because of Your leading. In Jesus' name, Amen.*

Real Self-Worth

Day 29

God made him who had no sin to be sin for us, so that in him, we might become the righteousness of God.
2 Corinthians 5:21, NIV

The self-esteem issue is very popular in educational circles. Educators blame most of students' problems on the lack of self-worth. However, the world's definition of healthy self-esteem and the perspective on the same subject from God's word differ greatly.

Jesus knew no sin. We knew no righteousness. But the Bible says that Jesus took on our sin so that we could take on his righteousness. WOW! When I made Jesus the Lord of my life, he took all my sin and I took his righteousness. That is not MY plan; it is God's. The world and educators in particular, think of self-worth as something to be achieved through accomplishment and respect from others. Good self-esteem, we are told, comes through belief in oneself and pride in oneself.

If our students gain self-esteem through pride in their accomplishments, opinions of others, or belief in themselves and their abilities, there is a fall waiting for them somewhere down the road. The only way for us to be strong and successful is for us to know who we are in Christ Jesus. Once we see ourselves the way Jesus sees us, no failure, trial, or rejection that life deals to us will have any effect on our self-worth. Once our students see themselves in Christ Jesus, they will stop running after the things of the world to make them feel good and look good.

Change the image on the inside of you today by seeing yourself the way Jesus sees you. Since we cannot share Jesus with students in public school, the Jesus they see in YOU will go a long way. Also, begin to pray that your students will find out who they are in Jesus and that they will stop trying to measure up to the world's standards.

Pray this prayer: *Dear God, I choose to believe Your word today. Your word says that I have been made the righteousness of God as I chose Jesus as Lord. I refuse to measure myself by the world's standards of success. I ask You to help my students to see who they are in Christ, and that any false sense of self-worth would be exposed and replaced by righteousness as a result of choosing Jesus. In Jesus' name, Amen.*

Not Number One

Day 30

Don't let anyone lead you astray with empty philosophy and high-sounding nonsense that come from human thinking and from the evil powers (the basic principles) of this world and not from Christ.
Colossians 2:8, New Living

Many people herald education as the number one answer to society's ills. Being educators we are particularly in danger of adopting this philosophy.

Let me make it clear that I am definitely not against education. I spent my career in education. But in some ways we have become a society of "educated fools." For instance, a tool of Satan was to get sex education into the schools. Now we have students everywhere that know about "safe sex" yet the rate of teenage pregnancy and sexually transmitted diseases is at an all time high. We have educated adults actually saying that the only way of keeping our young people safe and healthy is to educate them because "they are going to do it" anyway. What a cop out.

Education, while a good thing in perspective, is not the number one answer. Jesus Christ is the answer. The problems in our schools escalate, and we continue to stand by helplessly as more and more of our religious freedom is removed from our public places. But we are NOT helpless! Take steps today to promote prayer, Bible reading, and posting of the Ten Commandments in your school to the degree that the law allows. Get involved in the local politics of the matter. Pray for a spirit of repentance and revival in your school. At appropriate times, speak out in favor of Godly things in your school. Find out all the things the law will allow and help implement these in your school. There **will** be a noticeable difference.

Pray this prayer: *Dear God, thank You for opening our eyes to the deceptions of "education." Help me to model Jesus before my students in a way that they would desire to know Him and His ways. Show me how to get involved in returning the things of You back to our schools. Satan, you are a defeated foe. You will NOT have the lives our young people. Help us, Lord, as educators to put education into its proper perspective so that it accomplishes the most good. In Jesus' name, Amen.*

Constructive Criticism

Day 31

If you profit from constructive criticism you will be elected to the wise men's hall of fame. But to reject criticism is to harm yourself and your own best interests.
Proverbs 15:31,32, TLB

There have been times that my principal made helpful suggestions. Implementing these made me a more effective teacher.

How well do you take constructive criticism? Our first reaction generally is one of the flesh. We get offended. Do you know what the root of this reaction is? Pride.

The Word says that if a man of understanding is reproved that he will gain knowledge. Are you more interested in your pride or in becoming a better teacher for the benefit of your students? Take an inventory of these things and then make a quality decision to weigh the criticism given.

Constructive criticism generally comes from our superiors. Sometimes it comes from a good friend. Perhaps you are in a position that requires you to **give** constructive criticism at times. In all of these situations give fair thought to the suggestions given. Write them down. Meditate over them for a while. Do not let your flesh get in the way of implementing the suggestions. It is also a good idea to thank the person giving the suggestions. This will help create an even more positive working relationship and atmosphere. You will also gain knowledge and perhaps improve your method of teaching.

<u>Pray this prayer:</u> *Dear God, help me to receive constructive criticism with an open mind. I refuse to be offended when my superior offers suggestions and critique. Thank You for giving me creative ways to implement new suggestions. I choose to remain* *teachable and I want to be the best teacher possible for Your glory. In Jesus' name, Amen.*

Be Angry and Sin Not

Day 32

Better is a patient man than a warrior, a man who controls his temper than one who takes a city.
                              Proverbs 16:32, NIV

He who has knowledge spares his words, and a man of understanding has a cool spirit.
                              Proverbs 17:27, AMP

    Uncontrolled anger can be very destructive. The Bible has a lot to say about anger and with good reason. Although anger may be a natural initial reaction to some situations, it can be a trap of the enemy, the devil.

    An unfortunate incident occurred at a school where I taught. A new, young teacher quickly became frustrated by the behavior of his students. The students, sensing his lack of confidence and frustration, took advantage of the situation. Although many others and I offered advice on handling various student problems, he remained frustrated and ineffective. One day he became very angry in class and a scene ensued that caused his removal from the classroom.

    It was a very sad situation for a number of reasons. Those particular students went through two more teachers that year as the administration struggled to find substitutes to fill the position. This created inconsistency in the presentation of the subject matter, and the students' grades suffered. Other teachers on staff were assigned to cover that class in between substitutes, creating extra workloads for them. The young teacher suffered as a result of this incident, as his contract was terminated. Also, students in general, no matter the standards of their own behavior, expect teachers to be role models.

    We must remember that sin always has a ripple effect. Others are always affected by our sin. The Bible says to be angry and sin not. Today make a decision to walk after the Spirit and sin not.

Pray this prayer: Dear God, thank You for the blood of Jesus that took away my sin. However, I do not have to walk after the flesh and sin. I will stay in Your word and renew my mind and walk after the Spirit. Create a clean heart in me, O God, and renew a right spirit within me. By your power I will not give in to anger. In Jesus' name, Amen.

The Mouth

Day 33

A bit in the mouth of a horse controls the whole horse. A small rudder on a huge ship in the hands of a skilled captain sets a course in the face of the strongest winds. A word of your mouth may seem of no account, but it can accomplish nearly anything—or destroy it!
James 3:3-5, The Message

You set your course with your mouth. The third chapter of James discusses the mouth in depth. It can set you on a good course, or get you far off course.

It is so important to get control of our words. In Genesis God used words to create the universe. Since we are made in His image, we operate with the same capabilities. You can take a look at your life today, and wherever you are is predominantly because of what you have spoken into existence in the past. Most people are not aware of the power of words because sometimes the effect or result is not instant. But over a period of time, our words will set us on a course that will be like that of a ship: smooth sailing or into stormy winds.

Take time to study the whole third chapter of James. Use your mouth to set you on a course of God's best for you. Here are some things that God has said about you that you should start saying about yourself:

1. I am the righteousness of God in Christ Jesus. (2 Cor. 5:21)
2. I can do all things through Christ who strengthens me. (Phil. 4:13)
3. I am a cheerful giver. (2 Cor 9:7)
4. I have the mind of Christ. (1 Cor. 2:16)
5. The Holy Spirit teaches me all things. (John 14:26)
6. For God has not given me a spirit of fear, but of power, love, and a sound mind. (2 Tim 1:7)

Use your Bible and a good concordance to find out more about what God has said about you!

Pray this prayer: *Dear God, I believe what You have said about me. I believe that my mouth sets my course. Help me to change what I have been saying and instead say what the word says. Quicken me, Holy Spirit. Alert me instantly when I say things that do not line up with the word. I commit by the Spirit of God to change the way I talk. In Jesus' name, Amen.*

Student Destiny
Part One

Day 34

For I know the thoughts and plans I have for you, says the Lord, thoughts and plans for the welfare and peace, and not for evil, to give you hope in your final outcome.

Jeremiah 29:11, AMP

      At the beginning of each new school year I would have the same thoughts as a new crop of students filed into my room. Jeremiah 29:11 would be one of the main scriptures I committed to pray over them on a regular basis.
      Looking at modern day teenagers, it may be difficult at first to get this focus. They are so different from those of even a generation ago. (Did our teachers and parents say the same thing about us?) They dye their hair strange colors (even the boys!); they may have tattoos on their bodies; they may be wearing earrings in strange places; they may be wearing black fingernail polish and Gothic dress. But one thing is certain: God loves them all very much and has a very important plan and purpose for each and every one of them. Their destinies are in God's heart.
      I always ask God to help me see them as He sees them and to love them as He loves them. Sometimes it takes a while because our initial thoughts may be, "How could God use anything like ***that***?" But He can and He will. My job is to pray for them and to love them and to teach them. Maybe no one is praying out their destinies, and many of them do not even realize they have destinies. Commit to stand in the gap for them today by praying Jeremiah 29:11 over your students often.

Pray this prayer: *Dear God, I pray for the destiny that you have planned for my students. Satan, I plead the blood and say there is* *nothing you can do to stop the fulfillment of the plan of God for each and every one of them. I speak Jeremiah 29:11 over each and every one of them. Show me how to see them as You see them, Lord, and how to love them as You love them. In Jesus' name, Amen.*

Student Destiny
Part Two

Day 35

Who is there to condemn us? Will Christ Jesus, the Messiah, Who died, or rather Who was raised from the dead, Who is at the right hand of God actually pleading as He interceded for us?

Romans 8:34, AMP

While we are not to condone the negative behavior and manner of our students, it is so important not to condemn them either. I believe that so many of our young people are living with shame and condemnation, just crying out for someone to accept them as they are and to love them unconditionally.

Jesus' actions in the Bible are such wonderful examples of unconditional love. He was never the accuser of the people. I am in particular reminded of the woman caught in the act of adultery in John chapter eight. When Jesus invited those who were without sin to cast the first stone, of course they all left, because none of them were without sin. I believe that she became an avid follower of Jesus because of his unconditional love.

When you are tempted to condemn or accuse a student, remember the actions of Jesus and the woman in the story. He loved her and then he told her to sin no more. Jesus gave us the perfect pattern to follow to **restoration**, NOT **condemnation**.

Pray this prayer: *Dear God, help me to not be the accuser of my students. Help me love them back to restoration. Remind me often of the story of the woman caught in adultery. I come with the blood of Jesus against the shame in their lives. I thank You, God,* *that as I stand in the gap for them and love them unconditionally, You totally restore them. In Jesus' name, Amen.*

Joy Instead of Mourning

Day 36
…he will give beauty for ashes, joy instead of mourning, praise instead of despair.
Isaiah 61:3, New Living

My last years of teaching were spent in a public school of high quality. I was privileged to work in a place where the administration was committed, and morals, character, and principles were strongly encouraged by administration and faculty alike. Despite these good things, our students were not exempt from the problems of drugs, alcohol, and peer pressure.

One Monday morning shortly after arriving to school, we were called into an emergency faculty meeting. A young man, a student at our school, had committed suicide very early that morning at his home. We were all shocked and saddened. It was a very difficult morning as the rest of the students were informed and were offered counsel. Each of us as teachers could not help but wonder why we had not recognized the signs of impending tragedy.

At times like these, press into the Lord. He has promised that He will give beauty for ashes, joy for mourning, and praise instead of despair. He is our greatest comfort and his promises are not slack. Come to Him and sit in his lap and cry.

Begin also to get a new revelation of your role in praying over the things in your school. Through prayer so many attacks like this on our students can be thwarted. In fact, we probably have no idea how many times the devil and his schemes have been defeated through the power of prayer.

Pray this prayer: *Dear God, I need to run to You today and sit in Your lap and cry. Thank You so much for Your promises that bring* *me great comfort. I accept these promises by faith. I accept beauty for ashes, joy for mourning, and praise for despair. In Jesus' name, Amen.*

Safe in the Secret Place

Day 37

He who dwelleth in the secret place of the most High shall abide under the shadow of the Almighty.
Psalm 91:1, KJV

In recent times teaching has become labeled as one of the more hazardous and unpredictable occupations. Atmospheres of otherwise quiet study and deeper revelations of knowledge have become grounds to act out the violence whose thread is seen running through the media, computer games, and the internet. The addition of drugs and alcohol, and the subtraction of Biblical morals, principles and standards, set the stage for a volatile situation that awaits the right spark to ignite it. We have wonderful teachers that walk into the workplace day after day, wondering if some eruption will take place in their school.

Thank God that if we are born again that we do not have to live in fear! We can live in the secret place of safety. What a comfort it is to know that God has provided His children with protection from the evils of this world. The Bible is full of promises of God to protect His people from evil, but my favorite is the entire 91st Psalm. It says that we take refuge in Him. It says that no evil will touch our dwelling place. It says not to be afraid of the arrow that flies by day, (or, in modern day vernacular, the bullet!). It says He has given His angels charge over us! In fact, you cannot find any modern day danger that is not covered by the 91st Psalm. Talk about a book for all times!

Do not allow another day to go by without studying this powerful Psalm. Begin to pray it over yourself, your students, and your own children attending school. Believe what God has promised and refuse to waste time walking in fear. Instead, spend that energy joyfully doing the job God has called you to do.

Pray this prayer: Dear God, today I dwell in the secret place of the Most High. I abide under the shadow of the Almighty. I receive supernatural protection as Your angels take charge over me today. Thank You, Lord, that I do not have to walk in fear. I refuse to fear. A thousand may fall at my side but no danger will come near me. In Jesus' name, Amen.

Working Together

Day 38

Accept one another, then, just as Christ accepted you, in order to bring praise to God.

Romans 15:7, NIV

    I had the wonderful privilege of having a New York City teacher visit my Texas high school classroom. I was teaching a Bible History class in our public high school and she was very interested in implementing the course in schools in New York.

    My husband and I picked her up at her motel in our small Texas town. As we drove out to our ranch to show her around, we visited and became acquainted. At first, I had a hard time understanding her, just as she must have found it difficult understanding us. Our accents were quite different. Very soon, though, we were all laughing and talking.

    She visited in my classroom for two days. I was **so** blessed by Dorothy's presence. I could tell immediately that she loved the Lord. She asked lots of questions and we discussed lots of ideas. On her second day there I invited her to join Karen, my prayer partner, and me for our regular prayer meeting. It was a wonderful time in the Lord as we all prayed for each other and discussed the Scriptures together. The Holy Spirit moved mightily at lunch that day in my classroom. We were so different, and yet, came together, joined in Him perfectly. Dorothy said that although there were some differences between New York classrooms and Texas classrooms, we as teachers and part of the body of Christ shared with each other and loved each other. We still keep in touch today as if we had known each other all our lives. What a blessing to be a part of the body of Christ and joined together. If you do not know Jesus and are not a part of that body, get to know Him today!

<u>Pray this prayer:</u> *Dear God, thank You so much for the other members of the body of Christ. We need each other so much. Help* us to edify one another. Help us to encourage and strengthen one another. Help us to come together on common ground. Help us to walk in love toward one another and appreciate each other's gifts. In Jesus' name, Amen.

High Expectations

Day 39

And he began to give them his attention, expecting to receive something from them.
Acts 3:5, NASB

Do you have high expectations for your students, expecting them to perform on a higher level?

The man in the story in Acts 3 had been crippled from birth. He was carried to the temple every day to beg money from those going in and out just so he could "get by." He asked money of Peter and John, but there was so much more in store for him than that. Expectation was on both ends here. Peter and John knew that they could give him money and he would survive another day, but he would be left in the same general condition. As the crippled man and Peter and John released their faith, expecting something to happen, the power of God hit that man and it changed his whole life. Now he could earn his own living and not have to beg.

Your students in general are probably much more capable than they act or than you think. Our basic responsibility as teachers is to stretch them as far as they will go and then some. I was never much of a "read the chapter and answer the questions" type of teacher. I believed in projects and exercises in higher level thinking skills. And I found that despite their complaints and moaning and groaning at times, my students felt a great sense of satisfaction at the completion of a challenging lesson. Raise your expectations and prepare your students for a role in the bigger picture of life.

<u>Pray this prayer:</u> *Dear God, I want my students to be prepared for more than just today. Thank You for giving me teaching ideas that implement challenging lessons. Help me to find the middle ground between too easy and too difficult. As I raise my expectations for my students, help them to raise their expectations for themselves as* well. Holy Spirit, we welcome You as our teacher. In Jesus' name, Amen.

Go Ye

Day 40
And he said unto them, Go ye into all the world, and preach the gospel to every creature.
Mark 16:15, KJV

Each one of us as Christians has a calling to witness and spread the gospel to all the lost in the area in which we have been planted. Many times our lives and our actions should be enough to draw the lost to Christ without "beating them over the heads" with our Bibles. However, there are moments when God will ask us to do some bold witnessing. I remember one particular situation.

Many years ago before I rededicated my life to the Lord, I taught in a small Texas school. There was a very unpleasant incident that occurred between the mother of one of my students, and me. Shortly after that, I resigned and did not teach for a long while. During that period of time, the Lord changed me completely. Later, I took another teaching position in a nearby community. One day, several years into the job, a new janitor walked into my room. It was this woman. I had not seen her since the incident. At first I was taken aback, and I am sure she was too, and since neither one of us knew what to do, we just acted as if nothing had ever happened. Both of us were in a situation that could not be changed. The days, weeks, and months went by and every time she cleaned my room I told her what an excellent job she was doing, and we just started talking. I found that I really liked her.

Through our conversation I learned that she did not know the Lord. I knew God wanted me to share the gospel with her. I hesitated because of our pasts. Finally the day came, and I knew that I had to obey God. First, I asked her forgiveness for the long-past incident. We both cried, and she asked me to forgive her too. I shared the love of God and the gospel with her. We hugged. I would like to say that she received Jesus, but she did not. However, I obeyed God, and a seed was planted, clearing the way for another to come and reinforce that. (1 Corinthians. 3:6). I know she is coming into the kingdom at some point.

Is there someone in your world who does not know Jesus? Share with them today.

Pray this prayer: *Dear God, I will be obedient and share the gospel with whomever You put into my path. Prepare the hearts and open the ears to receive it. My heart cries for the lost. Give me the words to speak that they may hear. In Jesus' name, Amen.*

Press Toward the Mark

Day 41

I press toward the mark for the prize of the high calling of God in Christ Jesus.

Philippians 3:14, KJV

Notice that the above scripture says to "press toward the **mark**," not the **prize**. I had read this verse for years and always thought of reaching for the prize. But it does not say to reach for the prize, but press toward the mark. A good example of pressing toward the **mark** can be found in bowling. It would seem that one would aim the ball straight down the runway to knock all the pins down for a strike. But having taken one college class on bowling, I learned that there are arrows all along the beginning of the runway. Ideally, to make a strike, you should begin the roll of the ball on the arrows on the right if you are right-handed and on the left if you are left-handed. The ball should end up hitting in the middle of the pins for a strike. Another good example is in the game of golf. Rarely is the ball putted right at the hole because the green undulates, goes uphill, or goes downhill.

As teachers, there are so many times when it may seem as though we are not at all on the right track. But God's word says to press toward the MARK, and if we hit on the right marks we will naturally move toward the prize. Have the prize in your heart, but get your eyes on the mark. Move from mark to mark until goals are accomplished in your students.

Pray this prayer: Dear God, thank You for Your word that keeps me on track. Help me when I study the word to dig deeper and find what You have for me in it each day. I keep the prize in my heart and my eyes on the mark. Help me to hit the marks with each step I take, to Your glory and to the benefit of my students. In Jesus' name, Amen.

A Faithful Employee

Day 42

A faithful employee is as refreshing as a cool day in the hot summertime.

Proverbs 25:13, TLB

A faithful employee must have been difficult to find even in Solomon's time.

Here are some characteristics of a faithful school employee:

A faithful school employee

1. does not call in sick with some minor ache or pain.
2. does not call in sick and then vacation for a day.
3. is willing to come early and stay late.
4. does not miss duty time.
5. gives extra tutorial time when necessary.
6. prepares ahead for class.
7. supports the administration.
8. refuses to gossip.
9. helps other employees whenever possible.
10. is respectful of school property and equipment.

Faithfulness seems a rare commodity in our generation. Decide today to be faithful in your position at your school. God sees and He will reward.

<u>Pray this prayer:</u> *Dear God, I ask forgiveness for the times when I have not been faithful on the job. Show me the areas where I need to cultivate faithfulness. I know that when I am faithful my boss* *and my students will benefit more. Help me to model faithfulness for others around me. In Jesus' name, Amen.*

Idle Talk

Day 43

But I tell you, on the day of judgment men will have to give account for every idle (inoperative, non-working) word they speak. For by your words you will be justified and acquitted and by your words you will be condemned and sentenced.
Matthew 12:36, AMP

Every time I read this scripture I stagger. How many idle words come out of our mouths every day? There is a verse in Proverbs that says that idle talk leads to poverty. Our words along with our attitudes affect the whole environment of our classrooms and our relationships with our students.

It is so important to watch what we say. Obvious examples, of course, are things like profanity and coarse jesting (Ephesians 5:4; 2 Tim. 2:16). But have you ever thought about the common clichés that come out of our mouths that are so much a part of the death cycle? Here are a few:

"scared me to death"
"tickled me to death"
"laughed till I thought I would die"
"my feet (back, head, etc.) are killing me"
"blows my mind"

You are probably thinking, *"Well, people know that I don't really mean those things. They're just sayings."* **Words must be very powerful, or else Jesus would not have given the warnings in these verses.** God used words to frame the universe (Hebrews 11:3; Genesis 1:1-12), and we are created in His image and with the same power.

For one week, keep a journal of all the idle words that you speak. You will be very surprised. Make a commitment to change your words. If you fall back, just start over again. Come on over and live in the life cycle.

Pray this prayer: *Dear God, I see from Your word that words are powerful things. By the power of the Holy Spirit, make me aware of my words. I will not indulge in idle talk. Forgive me where I have done so in the past. I commit to changing the way I talk today, and I come over into the life cycle. In Jesus' name, Amen.*

Radically Blessed

Day 44

You will experience all these blessings if you obey the Lord your God: You will be blessed in your towns and in the country; you will be blessed wherever you go, both in coming in and in going out...the Lord will bless everything you do...
Deuteronomy 28:2,3,6,8, New Living

Blessed everywhere you go! That includes in your classroom. What would be some of the evidences of radical blessing in the classroom? How about your undisturbed peace and joy? How about all the supplies and equipment you need, regardless of the economic situation in your district? How about well-flowing lessons that target the information? How about joyful, happy students who are excited about learning? How about satisfied principals and superintendents?

If these conditions sound a little idealistic, it may a good idea to study the first fifteen verses of Deuteronomy. There are even **more** blessings listed. It might be a good idea to study the lives of Abraham, Isaac, Jacob, David and Solomon. Follow the lives of the kings who obeyed God, and read about the abundant blessings of God on them.

God wants to **radically** bless you. He wants you to walk in blessing everywhere so that you will be a blessing to someone else, especially your students. He has made provision for it. Read God's Word today and get a revelation of **His** idea of being blessed.

<u>Pray this prayer:</u> *Dear God, thank You so much for providing blessing for my life. As I seek Your face, and not just Your hand, reveal to me through Your Word Your idea of being blessed. I will* walk in Your commands and Your statutes. I receive the blessing of God as a free gift. In Jesus' name, Amen

Send Me?

Day 45

Also I heard the voice of the Lord saying, Whom shall I send, and who will go for us? Then said I, Here am I; send me.

Isaiah 6:8, KJV

    About halfway through my teaching career, I resigned my position, thinking that I would never return to teaching. Teaching had not been a pleasant experience for me. I had some terrible memories of the classroom.

    I decided to try doing some different things. I loved to sew, and so I started making wedding dresses and prom gowns. While I enjoyed this very much and had a lot of business, it just did not seem to bring the satisfaction that I had anticipated. At this same time I began to have a burning desire to get back to studying the Bible. For the past several years I had been in church, but I had not been growing in the Lord on my own. I started reading my Bible with new fervor. The Lord began to change me and show me many things which surprised and amazed me.

    At this time I was serving as the parent representative on the attendance committee at the local high school where my children attended. One day the principal approached me about a job teaching Spanish for the next school year. It had been two years since I left my last job. To be honest, I was very apprehensive about taking the job. I felt I had been a failure in the classroom in the past. But the next morning my ladies' prayer group laid hands on me and prayed and said that God was calling me to this "mission field". Suddenly I knew they were right. I knew that I would not be the same person that had been in that classroom the last time I taught. God was calling out my name and it was time to go. I knew that He would "cause me to triumph in Christ" (2 Corinthians 2:14) this time. My experience in the classroom for the remainder of my teaching career was absolutely fabulous!

Pray this prayer: *Dear God, help me to recognize You calling out my name. I yield myself right now and say that I am available to You. Send me! I go in the fervor and burning of the power of the Holy Spirit, determined to show Your light to a hurting, dying world. In Jesus' name, Amen.*

Stay Close and Go Far

Day 46

But seek ye first the kingdom of God, and His righteousness, and all these things shall be added unto you.

Matthew 6:33, KJV

Kingdom living is a very exciting journey! The Bible says that the kingdom of God is **within**, not in some far off place. How would you like for your life to reflect the kingdom every single day in every single area, especially in your classroom? The secret is simple: seek Him first!

As a teacher, I have awakened many mornings with a variety of school thoughts that range from getting lesson plans finished to pondering about the life of one or more of my students. At times it was difficult to focus on my time with the Lord instead of on all these issues. Then one morning God reminded me of the above verse. He reminded me that if I would seek Him first and stay close to Him, then all these other little things and issues would be solved. Our natural minds do not like a solution like that because we are too accustomed to trying to working things out ourselves.

To keep from being distracted, make a list of all the things that are trying to steal your attention (the devil comes to steal, kill, and destroy, John 10:10) from quiet time with the Lord. Lay your hands on and commit and roll the care of this list over on the Lord by saying, *"Lord, these are the things that need to be taken care of today. But I refuse to let thoughts of them interfere with our time together. Now, devil, I've written them down, and God and I both know what they are and you will not distract my prayer time with any more thoughts of them."*

You will find that your mind and heart will be clear and your time with the Lord unhindered by distractions. You will also find that every one of those things will be perfectly attended to in due time. Today stay close and go far.

Pray this prayer: *See above prayer inside of text.*

Man's Ways or God's Ways

Day 47

There is a way that seems right to a man and appears straight before him, but at the end of it are the ways of death.

Proverbs 16:25, AMP

Are you doing things man's way or God's way? Many times God's way will not make sense in the natural. For example, take the story of Noah. When God told Noah to build an ark, the people had never even seen rain. The Bible says that earth was watered from a mist coming out of the ground. Noah must have had some questions in his mind. But the Bible says that Noah was one of the few righteous left, so he must have been accustomed to following God, even when the instructions made no sense. What about the story of Joshua and the walls of Jericho? I do not know about you, but marching around walls seven times and shouting do not constitute normal war tactics that defeat enemies! But it worked! And then there is Abraham. God told him one night to get up and leave his family behind and go to a land that He would show him. Just like that!

Maybe God has shown you some unusual ways to deal with a student problem, employee problem, parent problem, or some other school issue. He may show you unusual ways to plan a class lesson or activity. If you have been spending ample time in fellowship with the Lord, you will recognize His voice when He tells you what to do. Even if the instructions seem unusual, remember the people in the Bible. They followed God instructions and came out on the other side in victory. You can too; just trust Him.

<u>Pray this prayer:</u> *Dear God, I trust that Your ways always work. Help me to have faith in Your instructions regardless of whether or not they make sense in the natural. I shut down my natural* *reasoning so that it will not interfere with receiving the perfect solution for my problem. After that, help me incorporate the instructions into the perfect plan for victory. In Jesus' name, Amen.*

Factor in the Anointing

Day 48
But you have an anointing from the Holy One, and you all know the Truth.

1 John 2:20, NIV

The anointing is simply the power of God on man. If you are a child of God, the Bible says that you have the anointing of God in you. That is a powerful statement! What that means is that in every situation you should come out victorious!

In and of ourselves, we can do nothing. But as born again, blood-bought children of God, we do not have to do anything in or of ourselves. Why operate in weakness when we have access to the power of God? Are you struggling with your students? Factor in the anointing! Are you struggling with your principal? Factor in the anointing! Are you struggling with your paycheck? Factor in the anointing! Are you struggling with a co-worker? Factor in the anointing!

Anoint actually means to rub all over, to smear into. It referred to an actual bodily oiling process done in the Middle East. Jesus said in Luke 4:18: **"The Spirit of the Lord is upon me, because he hath anointed me to preach the gospel to the poor; he hath sent me to heal the brokenhearted, to preach deliverance to the captives, and recovering of sight to the blind; to set at liberty them that are bruised..."** Even Jesus had to have the anointing on him to be powerful. We are called **Christians** because we are followers of Christ and can operate in that same anointing. Study your Bible today and begin to operate in the anointing that is available to you!

*<u>**Pray this prayer:**</u> Dear God, I am called and I am anointed by You. Thank You for anointing me. I receive the blessing of the anointing and I operate in it by the Spirit of God. I refuse to be defeated*

because I factor in the anointing in every situation. In Jesus' name, Amen.

Forever Settled

Day 49

Father, if you are willing, take this cup from me; yet not my will, but yours be done. An angel from heaven appeared to him and strengthened him.

Luke 22:42, NIV

Although Jesus was the lamb slain from the foundation of the world (Rev. 13:8), even **he** had to settle that decision once for all. Most people think, *Well, he's Jesus; he was ready for the cross. None of that process would be hard for him.* Wait a minute! The Bible says he CHOSE to be here in human flesh, to live as a man, here on earth, just like you and me (Phil. 2:7). And in the Garden of Gethsemane he asked his Father if there was any OTHER way to accomplish the goal of redeeming mankind.

We know he settled it once for all because a little while later, when he was arrested and circumstances started to get really hard, he tells Peter, "Do you think I cannot call on my Father and He will not at once put at my disposal twelve legions of angels (Matt. 26:55)?" Even Jesus had a choice to bail, to break and run, but he did not do that. Thank God he did not, or where would that have left all of us?

With each passing school year just functioning in the classroom becomes more and more challenging. I remember that one particular school year when God gave me the above scripture from Luke. When I had started the job it seemed I positively knew God had called me there. But as my classes and students became more difficult, I began to waver. I knew I had not settled once and for all that no matter what, I was staying put. As He brought that scripture to me one morning in prayer, I took my final stand and decided that **no matter what**, I was pressing on to the victory. Once you have heard from God, go to the Word and settle it forever. Your greatest reward lies in fulfilling His plan and purpose. Settle it, and when things get tough, you will not be moved.

Pray this prayer: _Dear God, I believe that You have called me to this school and classroom. I will look to You for every answer. I will not be moved by difficult circumstances. Until I hear differently from You, this is forever settled in my heart. In Jesus' name, Amen._

The Power of ONE

Day 50

Elijah was a man, just like us. He prayed earnestly that it would not rain and it did not rain on the land for three and one half years. Again he prayed and the heavens gave rain and the earth produced its crops.
James 5:17, 18, NIV

And who knows but that you have come to royal position for such a time as this?
Esther 4:14, NIV

    The Scriptures are full of examples of "ones" that made remarkable differences in situations, people, and circumstances simply by being obedient to what God had told them to do. Moses, Elijah, Esther, Nehemiah. Jesus. **Jesus.** He had a choice, but he went to the cross, and he purchased freedom for the rest of mankind. Oh, the power of **ONE**. Just one. Where would we be had Jesus not willingly given up his life? We would still be in the same sinful condition that ONE man Adam left us by his **disobedience.** I thank God that one person can make a difference.

    Look around your classroom. God loves every single one of those students. It doesn't matter what they look like, what they act like or where they came from; the Father loves them all the same. By the power of the Holy Spirit the love of God has been shed abroad in your heart (Rom. 5:5) and you can love them the same way. Through that love you have the power to make a tremendous impact on each and every one of their lives. Choose one of your most difficult students and ON PURPOSE begin to show the love of God in whatever way possible. By faith begin now to see each of your students through the eyes of Jesus, and as you move through the day attending to each one of them, know that God IS using you to help them.

Pray this prayer: *Dear God, today I put on my "Jesus glasses" to view each one of my students. I see them as victorious conquerors. I see them as overcomers. I see them loved by You. I see them as successful warriors in the army of the Lord. Help me today to guide them toward the destiny You have for them. In Jesus' name, Amen.*

Pray the Word
Part One

Day 51

So also is my Word. I send it out and it always produces fruit. It shall accomplish all I want it to, and prosper everywhere I send it.

Isaiah 55:11, TLB

Are you sometimes hesitant to pray for a student, not knowing exactly how to pray? Do you want to pray for students, being powerfully effective and getting it exactly right? You won't ever make a mistake when you pray the Word of God over them.

Many prayers appear in the Scriptures. Probably the most well known of them is the Lord's Prayer. Jesus used this when teaching the disciples how to pray. One part of that says, **" … Thy will be done, on earth as it is in heaven…"** When we pray God's Word, we are praying His perfect will. The Apostle Paul prayed some very powerful prayers found in Ephesians. I believe they are still powerful today and can be used to pray for our students. Here is a model from Eph. 1:16-19 and how you can pray it over your student:

"I do not cease to give thanks for _____ (name), making mention of him in my prayers: that You, the God of my Lord Jesus Christ, the Father of glory, may give to him the spirit of wisdom and revelation in the knowledge of You, the eyes of his understanding being enlightened that he may know what is the hope of Your calling what are the riches of the glory of His inheritance in the saints, and what is the exceeding greatness of Your power toward us who believe….."

Ephesians 3:14-20 are also Pauline prayers that are excellent to pray.

Praying the Scriptures allows you to pray the same thing over and over without the "vain repetitions." Since the Word is alive, every time you say or pray it, it is always new and fresh. If you do not know how to pray for a particular student or co-worker, go to the Bible today and make those ageless prayers your prayers.

Pray this prayer: *See above prayer and pray it, putting a name in the blank.*

Pray the Word
Part Two

Day 52

For I am watching over my word to perform it…
Jeremiah 1:10, NASB

Any scripture in the Bible can be tailored to pray over a student or other person. Some of my other favorite scripture prayers include Psalm 23, Psalm 91, Isaiah 54, Jeremiah 29:11, Eph. 6:10-17, and many others. Another Pauline prayer is this one from Colossians 1:9-14:

I do not cease to pray for _____ (name), and to ask that _____may be filled with the knowledge of His will in all wisdom and spiritual understanding; that _____may walk worthy of the Lord, fully pleasing Him, being fruitful in every good work and Increasing in the knowledge of God; strengthened with all might And according to His glorious power, for all patience and longsuffering with joy; giving thanks to the Father who has qualified _____to a partaker of the inheritance of the saints in the light. He has delivered _____from the power of darkness and translated _____into the kingdom of the Son of His love, in whom we have redemption through His blood, even the forgiveness of sins.

As you pray and release your faith, believe that God is working in that person's life. Connect your faith with the Holy Spirit as you pray these prayers. They are prayers you can pray over and over again, not only over students, but over yourself or a fellow teacher as well.

Pray this prayer: *Pray the above prayer over yourself or another person.*

The Wisdom of God

Day 53

Wisdom is the principal thing; therefore, get wisdom: and with all thy getting, get understanding.
Proverbs 4:7, KJV

But the wisdom that is from above is first pure, then peaceable, gentle, and easy to be entreated, full of mercy and good fruits…
James 3;17, KJV

What to do with students in certain situations requires wisdom, knowledge, and understanding. **Knowledge** is facts; **understanding** is knowing why, and **wisdom** is how to use knowledge.

Several years ago a troubled young man was in the senior English class that I was teaching. Large and overpowering, Mike always had an angry scowl on his face. He made every lesson difficult and many times refused to do assignments. I knew that his home life was not the best, and that no one in his family had ever graduated from high school. I tried every tactic I knew to discipline him, and make him pay attention, and desire to be successful in the class. One day after a particularly tense episode with him, I called him out into the hallway to try and talk with him. In the past, this had not been successful, but I just believed it was the thing to do. Suddenly I had an idea of just treating him as another adult and just being totally honest. "Mike, I know that you don't like studying **Macbeth** and that you see absolutely no reason to do so. I'll tell you something: I don't like teaching it either. But I signed my name to a contract and said I would teach you the material the best way I know how and I'm obligated to keep and honor that, whether or not I personally like it. Even though you don't like the material, maybe you could keep and honor your 'student contract' as well so you can pass and graduate." By the look on his face, I could tell that was a whole new concept for him. I never had any more trouble with Mike, and he was the first one in his family to graduate from high school.

    I know God provided me with that wisdom just when I needed it most. There is a way to deal with every difficult student you have. Tap into the wisdom from above today.

Pray this prayer: *Dear God, I know that there is a way to deal with every one of my students. I release my faith now to tap into Your wisdom concerning each one of them. The eyes and ears of my heart are open to receive that wisdom. May You be glorified in this. In Jesus' name, Amen.*

Creativity
Part One

Day 54

In the beginning, God created the heavens and the earth.

Genesis 1:1, NIV

God said, Let Us (Father, Son and Holy Spirit) make mankind in Our image, after Our likeness...

Genesis 1:26, AMP

Creativity in the classroom can make for interesting and exciting lessons. God is the God of creativity. Since you are made in His image, that creativity lives on the inside of you. This can be sharply developed if you walk with the Lord and follow the guidance of the Holy Spirit. Releasing this creativity into your lessons can have a powerful impact on the activities you are presenting to your students.

I was never much of a "read-the-chapter-answer-the-questions" type of teacher. I remember how boring that was when I was a student. Although there are isolated times when that must be incorporated, adventures in the classroom offer a method of learning that can take education to a higher level. Students can enjoy learning even difficult material. This also gives them a chance to develop their own creativity as they take part in lessons and activities that break out of the mold.

Developing plans for a creative activity sometimes takes more time and effort, but can be done with ease with the help of the Holy Spirit. Begin today taking your ideas out of the mold and up to another level into a creative place. The Holy Spirit is standing by to draw out the creativity placed by God on the inside of you.

Pray this prayer: Dear God, thank You for making me in Your image. I acknowledge that Your creative power lives on the inside of me. Holy Spirit, draw that out of me and guide me in developing interesting activities for my students. Help me plan each detail. I release my faith now in expectation. In Jesus' name, Amen.

Creativity
Part Two

Day 55

For we are His workmanship, created in Christ Jesus to do good works...

Ephesians 2:10, NIV

God has given me many creative ideas for the classroom. Teaching Spanish seems to automatically lend itself to interesting ideas. One year I thought it would be fun and educational to do a special Christmas project.

First, I asked my students to memorize several Christmas songs. They were required to say these into a tape recorder for a grade. (If they actually **sang** them, they received extra credit!) In between learning the songs, we read stories in Spanish about Christmas traditions in Mexico and Spain. Playing my guitar and also using the musical abilities of some of my more willing students, we formed a sort of Christmas choir. A few days before Christmas we took this choir to all three nursing homes in our town. It was wonderful to see the smiles on the faces of those senior citizens. Then we gave a performance in the lobby of one of the banks. The students enjoyed the activity immensely, and learned the material as well. When we returned to the school, some of the students' parents had provided hot chocolate and cookies, and we had a small celebration. The day before school was out for Christmas break, at the request of my principal, we went caroling up and down the halls. It was great fun, and none of us wanted to see it end. I decided to incorporate the idea every year.

Some years as a project we made piñatas. The students were two or three to a group and then based their ideas on stories we had read in class. Everyone loved doing the piñatas. Then, just before spring break, we had a big contest. I still remember the fun.

Modern technology can also lend itself to endless creativity. Power point productions, games and computer video production can all highlight classroom instruction.

God is NOT boring. He has an infinite amount of creative ideas for you. Begin to pray and release the creative ability in you and direct it toward your students.

Pray this prayer: *Dear God, show me creative ideas to use in my classroom. I know that the supply on the inside of me is exhaustless because You are an infinite God. Nothing is too hard for You. I open my eyes, ears, and heart to the creative ideas You have that are perfect my classroom and students. In Jesus' name, Amen.*

More Than Conquerors

Day 56

Yet amid all these things we are more than conquerors and gain a surpassing victory through Him Who loved us.

Romans 8:37, AMP

I was enjoying my Spanish Three class immensely one particular year. Spanish Three is always an advanced class and gives opportunity to really stretch the students and cover interesting territory.

Shortly after the school year began, one of the Spanish Two classes had to be divided because it had too many students. Because that class met during the Spanish Three period, and because the upper level class is usually smaller, my principal asked if I would take half of the students and teach Spanish Two and Spanish Three during the same period in the same classroom. To complicate matters further, the Spanish Two students were more challenging and somewhat of a behavior problem. In addition, my principal was planning to do my evaluation during this class period, in only a few weeks. Oh my!

My first thought was one of panic. Then I remembered all of the past situations where God had seen me through by His grace and mercy. I knew that this would be no different. Navigating this arrangement was at first very difficult. Between the two groups I would be running back and forth teaching, helping, guiding and correcting. I just continued to pray over the class each day, and in a couple of weeks things were running quite smoothly. Both classes did well and learned a lot. As I looked back, it did not seem nearly as difficult as I had first thought it would be…no wonder….I am more than a conqueror through my Lord Jesus Christ.

<u>Pray this prayer:</u> *Dear God, nothing can come into my life today that is too big for me to handle, because I am **more** than a conqueror* *through Jesus. Help me not to panic, but to step back and focus on You and Your infinite love and mercy. You will see me through anything that comes today. In Jesus' name, Amen.*

The Blessing of Friendship
Part One

Day 57

And Julius courteously entreated Paul and gave him liberty to go to his friends to refresh himself.
Acts 27:3, KJV

Friends can be refreshing! Who needs refreshing more than today's teachers?

One year our school counselor, a woman close to my own age, and I decided we both needed some fun time away from school and its pressures. We had known each other several years and had many things in common. We had taught each other's children, and worked together at the same school.

We decided to play golf every Wednesday afternoon after school. I was relatively new to golf, but she had been playing most of her life. We walked and carried our clubs, getting lots of exercise. We talked and laughed and had such a great time. Sometimes we shared particular prayer concerns about students or certain school situations, and that helped both of us. Although our golf wasn't all that great, and our motto was, "Just advance the ball," those times proved very refreshing as well as entertaining. One time a golf ball bounced off a tree and into the fairway where I was standing and hit me on the leg. It hurt and made a huge bruise, but we had another story to tell at school the next day! Other golf enthusiasts, such as our principal, assistant principal, and the golf coach found our stories entertaining as well. Many of us had great fun playing together in a school-wide tournaments, where we were not employers or employees but just friends.

I still remember those days with fond memories. Those times of refreshing with my school "family" not only helped ease the tensions many of us experienced during school hours, but also helped cultivate a different kind of appreciation for each other. I can imagine that the apostle Paul must have felt the same way. Relating to and interacting with your peers and friends at school may be just the refreshing you need today.

Pray this prayer: *Dear God, thank You so much for good friends! Help me to appreciate the people I work with and to be a blessing to them. Help us all to be times of refreshing for each other. By the guidance of the Holy Spirit, I will be a good friend. In Jesus' name, Amen.*

The Blessing of Friendship
Part Two

Day 58

Oil and perfume rejoice the heart; so does the sweetness of a friend's counsel that comes from the heart.
Proverbs 27:9, AMP

    Each day between classes we would stand across the hall from one another by our classroom doors. She was several years older than I. We went quite some time without doing much more than nodding. I judged her as not very friendly. I judged incorrectly.

    One day I had to ask Lavern a question concerning a matter of English grammar. After that we began speaking frequently and even standing in the hall visiting for more lengthy periods. I found her to be quite warm and soon we were beginning a friendship. Since both of us brought our lunches to school, we would sometimes eat together. As time went on, we ate together nearly every day in her classroom. I watched how she hugged students and genuinely cared for them. I began to seek her advice on certain student matters. Her counsel was very wise and greatly helpful in my classroom.

    For the next five years Lavern and I ate lunch together in her classroom. She poured into me many valuable elements and more or less became a mentor. She even invited me to her home on occasion. I was a single parent at the time rearing two small boys. Her husband would take them fishing and do other grandfatherly activities with them. She truly took me under her wing and I was a better teacher because of her input.

    Eventually those days came to an end, but I cherish the memories of a sweet friendship whose overflow touched all areas of my life, especially my classroom. I learned so much from Lavern about loving and caring for the students. Is there a mentor for you? Or maybe YOU are to BE the mentor.

Pray this prayer: *Dear God, is there a mentor for me? Or are You calling me to be a mentor? Thank You that counsel from a sweet friendship is so precious. Help me to notice where a mentor may be needed, or where I may find a mentor. Thank You for blessing my relationship with a friend. In Jesus' name, Amen*

To Come to the Rescue

Day 59

If you forbear to deliver them that are drawn unto death, and those that are ready to be slain; if you say, Behold, we knew it not, does not he that ponders the heart consider it? and he that keeps your soul, does not he know it? and shall he not render to every man according to his works?

Proverbs 24:11,12, KJV

Ginny enrolled in our high school during her junior year. I noticed in class that her face usually had a scowl on it, and she did not interact with the other students. She stayed mostly to herself. As the year progressed and she became more withdrawn, her grades began to suffer. One day I kept her after class and talked with her. It was obvious that she had deep emotional issues, not the least of which involved a negative home life. Over the next few weeks she came often after school to talk to me, or, she called me at home, and eventually, she told me that she was a lesbian. I hugged her and assured her that God loves her very much, and that He created her purposely as a woman to live out an exciting destiny as a woman.

My prayer partner and I prayed for her often during our meeting times. Ginny would come to both of us to talk sometimes, and we could tell that she was a very loving, caring person. She would voice concern about her younger brother and sisters at home. Although her grades finally improved enough for her to graduate the next year, her countenance revealed her continuing struggles.

After graduation Ginny continued to email and to call my prayer partner and me, and we would listen and pray with her. She was crying out for help. We knew that her answer lay in Jesus, who is the freedom from all bondage in this life. We continued to love her and present the Gospel to her. I haven't heard from her in a long while, but I believe seeds were planted, and I trust that at some point she will trust Jesus and receive him and total freedom. That will set her on a course of helping many others.

All around you are children that are in desperate need of rescue. Do not "forbear" (refuse) them every help possible and trust God to do the rest.

Pray this prayer: *Dear God, I know that only You can set people free. I know that You already provided freedom through the blood of Jesus on the cross. Help me to do my part to rescue the perishing and to trust You for the rest. I will not say, "Oh, I didn't know about that," when I see it clearly, In Jesus' name, Amen.*

Consider Eternity

Day 60

...He also has planted eternity in men's hearts and minds....

Ecclesiastes 3:11, AMP

In the mid-nineties I happened to catch the end of an intriguing television program. The people were discussing how the Bible could legally be taught in public school. My ears perked up immediately. I wrote down the phone number and called immediately for information. I was awestruck at the possibility of such a course being available and legal. How could it be? Considering all the hype about "separation of church and state," the thought had never crossed my mind that such a course would exist.

I received the information and decided to do some research on my own. First of all, I found that the clause "separation of church and state" is **NOT** in our Constitution. Many decades ago, certain courts took unjustified liberties and set precedents with those words of Thomas Jefferson's, words that had actually come from a letter he had written. Most of the general public, even some attorneys, are not aware of this. I also found that there were isolated school districts around the country that for decades had been teaching the Bible from a historical or literary perspective. Imagine my excitement!

I perused the information and found the curriculum to be very sound. I prayed about approaching my superiors with this information. My hope was that they would consider adding this elective course to our curriculum. Through the appropriate steps, my principal, superintendent, and school board scrutinized and approved the course, and it was added the following school year. The Bible as history and literature is still successfully taught today in that school and many others across the nation. Although it is very important to stay within the boundaries of the law, it is exciting to know that our students can be exposed to the most popular Book of all time.

I believe that at least part of God's plan for my return to teaching was to help implement this course. I was blessed to have taught the course for several years before leaving the classroom. I consider it an investment in eternity. How will you invest in eternity?

Pray this prayer: *Dear God, help me to invest in eternity. What better investment? Show me the ways to pray, the decisions to make and the steps to take to do this. I receive Your guidance today. Pave the way that I will need to go. In Jesus' name, Amen.*

Manifestations of the Holy Spirit

Day 61

...and He has filled him with the Spirit of God, in wisdom, in understanding and in knowledge and in all craftsmanship; to make designs for working in gold and in silver and in bronze and in cutting of stones for settings, and in carving of the wood, so as to perform in every inventive work. He also has put in his heart to teach, both he and Oholiab...

Exodus 35:31-34, NASB

    It is sad that the moving of the Holy Spirit is strange and foreign to us, especially in such a day and hour as this. I believe this stems from expecting something weird to happen when the Holy Spirit manifests. Our experiences with the Holy Spirit should be **regular and anticipated** occurrences in our daily lives. When we receive Jesus as our Savior, the Holy Spirit comes to live inside us, but the Bible also speaks of His presence coming ON us.

    In the above scripture notice how normal it was for the Holy Spirit to come upon these workers to do the jobs they had been called to do for completion of the tabernacle. These were just ordinary workers made EXTRAORDINARY in their tasks because the Holy Spirit showed up on the scene. There was nothing weird about it; He just manifested Himself to help them accomplish the very best work possible. I also found it interesting that the Holy Spirit put it in their hearts to TEACH. So many times the Holy Spirit has manifested Himself in my classroom and turned everything in a different and much better direction.

    If we know Jesus as our personal Savior, the manifestation of the Holy Spirit is available at any time needed. One reason we have not experienced this on a greater level is because we have not invited Him to manifest Himself at any given time in our lives. Another reason is that we have not done the things that increase sensitivity to moving of the Holy Spirit. Get into the Word and read about all the places where the Holy

Spirit manifested on ordinary people to give extraordinary power. Check out these places in the Bible: Numbers 11:25,26; Judges 15:15, 16; 1 Sam. 16:13; 2 Sam. 23:2; Micah 3:8; Matt. 12:18; and many other places. The Holy Spirit is our helper in the classroom (and any other job for that matter), so let Him help today!

Pray this prayer: *Dear God, thank You for the gift of the Holy Spirit. Holy Spirit, I invite you to manifest in my life at any time, in any way. God, help me to become more sensitive to the moving of the Spirit. In Jesus' name, Amen.*

Do Not Neglect Training

Day 62

Listen to my instruction and be wise; do not ignore it.
Proverbs 8:33, NIV

Training students to listen and closely follow instructions is so important. The Bible has a lot to say about this, especially in Proverbs. In this powerful book wisdom is touted as bringing us into health, wealth, and delight. Failure to listen well and follow instructions can result in many unnecessary setbacks. Teachers can be instrumental in training students to listen well and follow instructions.

One year one of my Spanish classes was extremely large, having the most students I had ever had during one class period. Rows of desks were wall to wall. There was hardly space enough to move around the room. I knew from experience that discipline and structure would be very important if any learning was to take place in this situation. Since this period was only fifty minutes long, I had to make the most of each minute. I knew the students must be trained to listen so I would not have to repeat and consume precious time. One of the trouble spots seemed to be the escalating activity as the period drew to a close. I would try to gain their attention to close the lesson properly, but my attempts were unsuccessful.

One day I had a great idea. Since this class period was right before lunch, I decided to make that work in my favor. I told my students that five minutes before the lunch bell, I would open the door into the hall and that would be the signal to settle down, get quiet, and await last instructions as to homework or other matters. If there was not total quiet and settling, I would keep the class five minutes into the lunch break. It worked fabulously! I only had to keep them a couple of times before they were totally trained! No matter how active the class became during a project or drill, all I had to do was open that classroom door and I had immediate quiet and attention.

There are brilliant ideas waiting for you as well. Use them to train your students to listen and pay attention.

Pray this prayer: *Dear God, thank You for the wisdom in your Word. I desire to train my students to listen and obey. Help me to incorporate brilliant ideas to get their attention. Help me teach my students to listen and follow instructions. In Jesus' name, Amen.*

Cast Your Care
Part One

Day 63

Cast your cares on the Lord and He will sustain you...

Psalm 55:22, NIV

Whether you are a new teacher just starting out, or a veteran teacher familiar with classroom ways, the 21st century classroom activity will attempt to wear you down.

This is unlike many other jobs because it is such a great responsibility to have a part in molding young minds. Preparing lesson plans, tests, imparting information and grading papers were often the easiest part of the job. Meeting each student's deeper needs that manifest themselves as classroom problems is the real challenge. I would find myself bringing home every worry and care of each one of them. It was so overwhelming. How could I meet every need? There were so many.

Then I found this scripture. When I read and studied this, it set me free with the realization that Jesus must love and care for the children much more than even I do, and that he provides for their care. Also, I began to realize that there is only so much I can physically do to improve their lives; God must do the rest. While I can pour myself into the things I **can** do, and also pray for them, it does no good to worry about what I cannot do. So I cast the cares of it all on to Jesus and fully trust.

It helps to physically go through the motions of symbolically casting the care. Take a wadded up piece of paper and speak the cares onto to it. Then literally cast it into a wastepaper basket and believe that it is done. Do not let it enter your mind again, becoming a care once more. God loves you and those students so much, and He can do a much better job of attending to them and their needs.

Pray this prayer: Dear God, thank You that Jesus died on the cross in order to take my cares. Only He is qualified to bear them because of his broken body and shed blood. I determine to cast my cares on Jesus and not pick them up again. I do this by the power of the Holy Spirit and I find great freedom in doing so. In Jesus' name, Amen.

Cast Your Care
Part Two

Day 64

If you will humble yourselves under the mighty hand of God, in his good time he will lift you up. Let him have all your worries and cares, for he is always thinking about you and watching everything that concerns you.
1 Peter 5:6,7 TLB

Casting the whole of your care is a humbling experience. It is prideful to think that we can do everything ourselves without God's help. If so, for what reason did Jesus go to the cross? This whole passage together lets us know that as we release our cares and anxieties on to Jesus that we are humbling ourselves. It says that in due time we will be lifted up. Certainly our positions as educators offer many opportunities for walking in humility and casting our cares.

When we walk in humility, we are submissive one to another (Eph. 5:21). We do this out of reverence for Christ. It may mean recognizing someone as more knowledgeable than you are. One year I had a woman assigned to me to do her student teaching in my Spanish classes. She was a beautiful Hispanic woman who was close to my age and had just completed her college courses. I was so apprehensive because her native language was Spanish, and I felt inadequate to have **her** learning from **me.** I purposely cast that care on the Lord. I decided to humble myself and speak frankly to her. She was so kind and gracious; we decided that I could learn more about the language from her, and that she could learn more about teaching strategies from me.

As it happened, we had a fulfilling semester. We had lots of fun and gained many things from one another. I taught her about being a teacher, and she imparted more to me about Spanish. She also was a very creative person, and I allowed her freedom to use that with the students as well. We were "submissive one to another." The semester came to an end much too soon. God **IS** always watching what concerns you and if you humble yourself and turn all over to Him, success will be the result.

Pray this prayer: *Dear God, today I humble myself under your mighty hand and I receive your promise of lifting me up. Show me the places where I have not cast my cares on to You. I choose humility over pride and I walk in the best You have for me. In Jesus' name, Amen.*

Knit Together

Day 65

That their hearts might be comforted, being knit together in love…

Colossians 2:2, KJV

Many of our students today come from dysfunctional families. Teachers observe the repercussions of this sad fact. We all know that family life is very important to the overall development of any person.

At our high school we decided that it could be very beneficial to students to implement a program that mimicked the family setting. Each teacher was assigned six to eight students to be a family group for the school year. Every week the family groups met in the teacher's classroom for around thirty minutes just to discuss things and bond. We teachers were also encouraged to have other interaction with our "families" throughout the rest of the week.

The first meetings were strained and difficult. No one wanted to talk, and some students had issues with some of the other students and resented being in a "family" group with them. I would attempt to draw them out but to no avail. During the little time that I was able to get them to talk, I discovered heartbreaking things about their backgrounds. I felt deep compassion for them. I suppose that I had always taken for granted a strong, stable family life.

I began to pray for each of them and for our "family." I knew the idea had promise. Since I lived only a few blocks from school, one day I invited them all to lunch at my house. My husband and one of his friends did the cooking, and we all sat down around the set table together. My husband offered prayer over the meal and all of us. We all sat together eating and talking and laughing, just as a real family would. It was fun. From that time on we all got along much better, and our family group meetings improved. Family is God's idea and a most remarkable thing!

Pray this prayer: *Dear God, thank you so much for families! I realize that it is not Your will for families to be broken and dysfunctional. Help me to stand in the gap for students who have a no family life and show me how to be "family" for them. Help me to show the love of Jesus to them in unique ways. Restore families in this nation. In Jesus' name, Amen.*

Are You A Fruit-Bearer
Part One

Day 66

A certain man had a fig tree planted in his vineyard, and he came looking for fruit on it, but did not find any. So he said to the vinedresser, See here! For these three years I have come looking for fruit on this fig tree and I find none. Cut it down; why should it continue also to use up the ground—that is, to deplete the soil, intercept the sun and take up room?

Luke 13:6,7, AMP

Getting the most out of any job requires putting the most into it. Teaching, especially, is a calling that one must thoroughly give into in order to be successful. One day I overheard a remark made by someone who obviously is not a teacher.

"Teachers have it so easy. Just come in every day, eight to three, assign the chapter with the questions and sit at your desk and do crossword puzzles. Summers and holidays off! Turn in a few grades now and then there you have it!"

That is the view many outsiders have about teachers, but the ones I know are very hard workers. I believe that most teachers are not just "taking up room and depleting the soil," because the children would be the real losers in that situation. But the comment did cause for reflection about being a fruit-bearer not just in the classroom, but also for the kingdom of God. A main reason we are here on this earth is to do the job that God called us to do, and that requires bearing fruit. In the passage above it was recommended that the tree not bearing fruit be cut down. In order to bear fruit, we must realize that our connection as the branches to the Vine (John 15:5) is vital and opens the way for the sap of Holy Spirit to flow through us. In this way MUCH fruit is produced.

Take some time to meditate today about your purpose in the classroom and in the kingdom. Make a conscious decision to be a fruit-bearing tree.

Pray this prayer: *Dear God, I know you have me on this earth and in this classroom for a specific purpose. I do not want to simply "take up room and deplete the soil." Holy Spirit, work in me to produce fruit where I have been planted. In Jesus' name, Amen*

Are You A Fruit-Bearer
Part Two

Day 67

But he replied to him, Leave it alone, sir, just this one more year, till I dig around it and put manure on the soil; then perhaps it will bear fruit after this, but if not, you can cut it down and out.
Luke 13:8,9 AMP

And these are they which are sown on good ground: such as hear the word, and receive it, and bring forth fruit....
Mark 4:20, KJV

    Key to being a rich fruit-bearer is receiving the Word of God deep into the rich soil of your heart and allowing it to do its work there. The vinedresser recommends "digging around it" (the soil), and "putting manure" (faith) on the soil. Then it is ready for the seed (the Word).

    When a farmer plants his crop, he doesn't just get up one day and decide to go throw a little seed out and see what happens. He ***plans*** for planting day because he is expecting a large fruit crop. I have watched my farmer husband do this for years. First he removes any rocks or other debris out of the field. Then he prepares the soil by plowing it several times. Then the rains come and he may plow again. After this he fertilizes and perhaps applies weed killer. Then one day conditions are just right and the ground is prepared to receive the seed. He plants on that day.

    When we open ourselves up to the Holy Spirit to dig around the soil of our hearts, then preparation is made to receive the Word, or the seed. The catalyst, (or manure), faith, puts everything into motion. By reading and meditating in the Bible (Psalm 1; Joshua 1:8), the Word, or seed, is planted in our prepared hearts. By the power of the Holy Spirit the Word produces mightily, showing us how and what to do in the classroom at just the right times. Then there will be fruit on the vine and a great harvest!

Pray this prayer: *Dear God, I offer my heart up to You, to be plowed by the Holy Spirit, and prepared as good ground to receive the seed, Your Word. As the Word grows in the prepared soil of my heart, it guides me in the classroom and my students partake of the fruit produced through me. In Jesus' name, Amen.*

Are You A Fruit-Bearer Part Three

Day 68

Yes, I am the Vine; you are the branches. Whoever lives in me and I in him shall produce a large crop of fruit. For apart from me you can't do a thing.

John 15:5, TLB

…bearing fruit in every good work,…

Colossians 1:10, NASB

As a teacher, how can I be certain that I am bearing fruit? Is it when my students pass a test? Is it when the light dawns on their faces and I know they understand a concept? Is it when they successfully complete a project? Is it when they come back years and years later and say thank you for what they learned from you? Or is it when one of your students in Spanish class who seemed the least enthusiastic graduates from college as a Spanish teacher? One day as I pondered all of this, I found none of these answers satisfactory. I decided to take a walk and talk to the Lord about it, because I wanted to KNOW that certainly that I am bearing fruit.

As I walked, I reflected on many other instances in my teaching experience. One time a teacher from the classroom next door told me that her son, a student in my Bible History class, was overheard in a restaurant after a baseball game talking with some of his fellow players. They were discussing the Bible and my Bible History class. Apparently the conversation was quite lively. "That has to be it!" I thought to myself. But the quiet voice of the Lord said, "No, that is not it." I continued my walk, just listening for more of His voice.

When I returned home, I had an urging to look up all the verses in the Bible on *fruit.* The moment I read the above verse, John 15:5, I knew I had found the answer! Since Jesus is my Savior, He lives **IN** me. Since I follow after Him with all my heart by obeying his commands, I live **IN** Him. Therefore, **WHATEVER** I do bears much fruit, whether inside the classroom or out. I KNEW THAT WAS THE ANSWER! It was a comforting answer that brought great freedom, because in teaching, we may never "see" much of our fruit. However, if we meet the conditions of the above scripture, then by faith we are "bearing fruit in every good work." That's good news!

*<u>**Pray this prayer:**</u> Dear God, I believe that I am in You, and You are in me, and that I bear fruit in every good work. If I am not meeting these conditions, help me Lord to truly know You and follow hard after You so that I will bear fruit in every area of my life. In Jesus' name, Amen.*

The Mercy of God
Part One

Day 69

The Lord is gracious and full of compassion, slow to anger and abounding in mercy and loving-kindness.
Psalm 145:8, AMP

Many years ago I taught in a very small school that housed kindergarten through the twelfth grade. I remember an incident that makes me think of the mercy God has toward us.

There was a television and a VCR sitting on a rolling cart that was parked out in the hallway. After recess one day, a little third-grade boy came running inside the door and into the hallway and collided with the ill-placed cart, accidentally knocking it over. The television smashed to pieces and the VCR was demolished as well. He stood still in shock, and then burst into tears, knowing something valuable had been destroyed. Startled by the unusually loud noise and commotion, his teacher ran out of his classroom and into the hallway. There stood the little boy, crying and near hysteria. Broken pieces and parts lay everywhere. A kind man of many years' experience, the teacher quickly sized up the situation, walked over to the boy and drew him into a hug. As the little boy began to try and explain, the teacher reassured him with kind, comforting words until the sobs subsided. He did not chastise him at all.

This little boy was new in the district and was being reared by his recently- divorced single mother. So many changes had occurred for him, and moving to a new school was just one more in a long line of transitions. At a crucial time in his life, a positive male role model showed mercy and did exactly the right thing to add stability and confidence to this young boy's life. Shortly his mother arrived on the scene, summoned from her classroom. She took her son in her arms and hugged him tightly. There were no repercussions, and the boy's mother never forgot the impact that teacher made during an extremely difficult time in her son's life.

I am that boy's mother.

Pray this prayer: *Dear God, thank You so much for Your mercy. Where would we be without it? Help me to understand Your mercy. Help me to see it in all the areas of my life. You are truly a merciful God. In Jesus' name, Amen.*

The Mercy of God
Part Two

Day 70

...*he does not treat us as our sins deserve or repay us according to our iniquities.*
$$\textit{Psalm 103: 10, NIV}$$

For as the heaven is high above the earth, so great is his mercy toward them that fear him.
$$\textit{Psalm 103:11, KJV}$$

Some of the writing in this book has been devoted to discipline and its role in the classroom. I cannot stress enough the importance of discipline in establishing and maintaining proper order in the school room. Without it there would be chaotic confusion, and learning would be minimal. However, we must be sensitive to the times when situations with students call for mercy.

I recall a particular time with a student. He was a senior and was in one of my Spanish classes. He was on the verge of failing. Though not a behavior problem, I could tell that he was regularly distracted. But I also had reason to believe he was bright; he was simply not performing. I had sent out failing slips and made him aware of the seriousness of the situation. Time grew shorter and shorter and three weeks before graduation I called him in for one last conference and told him that he would most likely not graduate because he was on the verge of failing my class. He sat quietly for several minutes.

"Mrs. Kiesling, please, is there anything I can do to pass? I have been working two jobs because my girlfriend is pregnant and we are getting married. I know my school work has suffered, but I have to graduate so I can go to work." I told him that I would have to think about it and for him to return the next day. As I prayed, I knew what I should do.

I outlined several assignments of extra work. He satisfactorily completed these and graduated. It was not what I initially wanted to do. It was not what he "deserved." But then I remembered and was so glad that I did not get what I deserved many times in my life. God is so merciful and He wants us to show mercy too.

Pray this prayer: *Dear God, thank You for Your mercy in my life. Help me, Holy Spirit to show mercy to others. Help me as a teacher to discern between times to discipline and times to be merciful. As I grow in You, God, these things are made clear to me. In Jesus' name, Amen.*

From the Head
Part One

Day 71

How wonderful it is, how pleasant, when brothers live together in harmony! For harmony is as precious as the fragrant anointing oil that was poured over Aaron's head, that ran down his beard and onto the border of his robe.

Psalm 133, New Living

Aaron was the brother of Moses and the high priest. He was a leader and the people were to follow his example. Everything that he did was passed right down to the least of the people. As long as Aaron made the right decisions and everyone followed, order and harmony abounded.

Harmony starts at the head and requires the cooperation of all. The head of the school district is the superintendent, and the head of your school is the principal. It is so important that we, as teachers, make every effort to support these in charge. Some of my most pleasant teaching years occurred under the leadership of a particular principal and vice principal twosome. Order and discipline were tantamount with these men in charge. They had been close friends for many years and worked very well together to create an atmosphere of unity for our whole high school staff. We called them The Dream Team. They were held in high respect. We may not have agreed with their every decision, but we knew they always had our best interests at heart. Knowing we could count on their backing made our jobs in the classroom much easier. The students also sensed the strength of this team and knew and respected the boundaries. As all of the teachers gave their loyalty and support, the "anointing" that started from the head affected every one of us. This allowed us to work with one another toward the common goal of what was best for our students.

Perhaps the administrator over you is very difficult. It is still very important to support this person and submit to him. God will honor this in you. Begin to pray diligently for him. Remember that many times we are not privy to information that is delegating circumstances, and we should not make judgments. Just continue to honor God by your submission. Your prayers will affect the anointing that is flowing down so that all may function in harmony.

Pray this prayer: *Dear God, help me to honor you by submitting to the administrators in charge over me. Teach me how to pray effectively for them. Help them to be strong leaders that do the right thing so that the anointing flows down to benefit all. In Jesus' name, Amen.*

From the Head
Part Two

Day 72

I exhort therefore, that, first of all, supplications, prayers, intercessions, and giving of thanks, be made for all men; for kings, and for all that are in authority, that we may lead a quiet and peaceable life in all godliness and honesty.

1 Timothy 2:1,2, KJV

One year I sponsored a group of students on a trip to Washington D.C. One of my college-aged sons accompanied me as well. This was a very special trip because it would include attending the inauguration of the first term of President George W. Bush.

We arrived one week prior to the inauguration and spent those days seeing all the marvelous sights in Washington. The atmosphere was charged with excitement as all kinds of special events took place in honor of the incoming president. I will not soon forget the Smithsonian, the war memorials, the Supreme Court building, the Library of Congress or my favorite, Ford's Theater. Of course, inaugural day itself was very exciting as we stood on Pennsylvania Avenue watching the parades and stretch limos go by carrying important guests. The day before the inauguration my son and I walked to the White House. We had not been able to take a tour because it had closed for security reasons. We were surprised that it was relatively quiet around there. We decided to walk around it and in front of it and pray for the incoming president. It was a great time.

We are given the command in First Timothy to pray for the leaders of our nation. They have very difficult decisions to make that affect all of us. They are the leaders and all they do flows down to us. Our prayers are important because the Bible says that **"righteousness exalts a nation"** (Proverbs 14:34). Proverbs 29:2 says, **"When the righteous are in authority, the people rejoice, but when the wicked beareth rule, the people**

mourn." It is our responsibility not just to pray, but to vote and put righteous people in office. Make this a priority today and always!

Pray this prayer: *Dear God, I lift up the leaders of our nation today: our president, every senator, congressman and judge. I plead the blood of Jesus over them. Help them to make decisions that agree with Your word. Open the eyes of their hearts that they would not be deceived. In Jesus' name, Amen.*

Diligence

Day 73
Lazy people don't even cook the game they catch, but the diligent make use of everything they find.
Proverbs 12:27, New Living

    In the dictionary, one of the meanings of the word **diligent** is <u>industrious</u>. To impart knowledge and keep lessons interesting, teachers must definitely be industrious. One year I was looking for something new and interesting for my Spanish classes. In my Bible History class one of my students had brought to school a parallel English/Spanish Bible to show to me. I suddenly had an idea. I went to my principal and asked if I could use that book in my Spanish classes. He gave me permission to do so.

    It was actually fun to prepare the lessons. There were so many things I could do! I decided to use the story of Moses and the Exodus. First I created a list of vocabulary words. These words were some that we had no exposure to in our textbooks. Learning these new words was fascinating even for me. I also created lessons on verb tenses. Then we read the story aloud, and I wrote objective questions in Spanish as homework for the students. We discussed the story in Spanish. Ultimately we had a test. Since we used the parallel English/Spanish Bible, the students were able to better grasp new word meanings. We were able to find a Spanish copy of the then popular movie **Prince of Egypt**. The unit took about three weeks. At this point my plans were to move on to other material in our texts, but the students begged for another unit. I decided we could cover the story of David and Goliath and still have time to finish requirements in our texts before the end of the year.

    What great lessons these turned out to be! We all learned a lot. Take what you have and be industrious or, diligent in your classroom. Ask the Lord to show you what interesting tools you have at hand.

Pray this prayer: Dear God, I want to use everything I have at hand to impart knowledge to my students. Help me to recognize interesting ideas when they present themselves. I will be diligent and industrious in using them to create my lessons. I yield myself to the Holy Spirit to do this. In Jesus' name, Amen

Covered and Protected
Part One

Day 74

I have given you authority to trample on snakes and scorpions and to overcome all the power of the enemy; nothing will harm you.

Luke 10:19, NIV

And they overcame him (Satan) by the blood of the Lamb, and by the word of their testimony...

Revelation 12:11, KJV

    Educators everywhere will not soon forget that April day of the Columbine shooting. A thousand miles away from Colorado, I remember the atmosphere of our entire Texas school that day. It was very sobering. In the few years following, other similar incidents occurred. How could teachers or students any longer feel safe in a school setting? By the power of the blood of Jesus.

    It is so important to have revelation about the blood of Jesus and how to apply it. In the Old Testament the blood of animals was used to cover the sins of the people. In Exodus chapter twelve we find the story of the children of Israel putting lamb's blood on the doorposts to be protected against death of all of the firstborn. That is a picture of what was to come in the New Testament when Jesus shed his blood on the cross. The blood of Jesus is at the very core of our salvation. We were bought with his blood. What a precious price to pay! But now we have access to the blood and its role in our protection. We can plead the blood of Jesus over our lives or over any situation that requires great power or protection. The blood represents everything Jesus is and all he has done for us.

    Other verses about the blood of Jesus include: 1 Peter 1:18-20; Colossians 1:12-14; Ephesians 1:7; 1 John 1:7; Romans 5:9; Hebrews 10:19, 22; and Ephesians 2:13. Study these and find out more about the blood of Jesus so that you can know what the blood purchased for you.

Pray this prayer: *Dear God, thank You for sending Jesus to die and shed his blood for me. Holy Spirit, teach me about the blood of Jesus and how to apply the blood scriptures to my life and circumstances. In Jesus' name, Amen.*

Covered and Protected
Part Two

Day 75

Through faith he (Moses) kept the Passover, and the sprinkling of the blood, lest He that destroyed the firstborn should touch them.
                                    Hebrews 11:28, KJV

So how do we sprinkle or "plead" the blood of Jesus? With our words that are released in faith! Not mechanically, or by a formula, but with faith-filled words. It's that simple!

My friend, Bible teacher and author Glenn Smith, tells this story in his book, **Our Lives Are In His Blood** :

"Living alone in her apartment in Austin, Texas, our daughter had retired for the night. She was sound asleep when awakened by a pressure on her throat. Startled, she opened her eyes to see a grown man straddling her on the bed. He was holding a knife to her throat so fiercely that when she endeavored to open her mouth to scream, she could not. She finally managed to croak out in a faint whisper, 'I plead the Blood.'

'What did you say?' the man yelled at her while loosening the pressure on her throat.

Finding her voice, she said loudly, 'I plead the Blood!'

'Don't say that word!' The man screamed in terror and totally removed the knife from her throat. The man leapt off the bed, headed for the door.

She got up and ran after him screaming, 'The Blood, the Blood!' The man ran out into the street with her following him and yelling, and he ran right into a police officer who apprehended him." **(Our Lives Are In His Blood, p. 38, 39)**

Plead the blood of Jesus in faith. You can do this over situations, circumstances, people, places and things. Study what the Bible says about the blood. There's power in the blood of Jesus!

Pray this prayer: Dear God, I plead the blood of Jesus today over myself. I plead the blood of Jesus over my classroom, the school building and my students. As I sprinkle the blood in faith over every area of my life, I believe that I am protected and kept. In Jesus' name, Amen.

The Sin of Pride

Day 76

Do not let any unwholesome talk come out of your mouths, but only what is helpful for building others up according to their needs, that it may benefit those who listen.

Ephesians 4:29, NIV

Never slander a person to his employer...
Proverbs 30:10, New Living

    I once knew of a teacher who was called into the principal's office for a conference following the routine classroom evaluation. As the teacher and the principal were discussing the evaluation, the principal would add his praise of what a great teacher he believed this person to be. As they were talking, the teacher at first thanked him but then began to tell of another teacher she knew that really didn't care about the students, who just did as little as possible to get by, and other things of the same nature. No names were mentioned. After a few more comments, the teacher and the principal concluded the conference. Later that evening, this teacher began to really come under conviction because of the comments made about the other teacher, even though no names had been mentioned. This teacher realized that she had not only made that person look bad to the principal, but had also made herself look bad by behaving in this way. She also realized that upon hearing the principal's praise of her own abilities, she had allowed pride to lead her into sin. First, she repented before the Lord and asked forgiveness. The next day she went to the principal and asked his forgiveness also, telling him that she had been wrong in making those comments and judgments about another person on the staff.

    Remembering that it takes all our gifts to make school successful will help to keep you out of pride about your own accomplishments in the classroom. Judging one another, and in particular, voicing these judgments to others will not only harm people but reflect on you as well. Exhort and encourage one another at every opportunity.

Prayer this prayer: *Dear God, I value the gifts that You have put into every teacher. Help me to appreciate each staff worker. Give me encouraging words that help and exhort others each day. I choose not to make judgments or slander any one of them. In Jesus' name, Amen.*

A Different Look At *Joy*

Day 77
...*be not grieved and depressed, for the joy of the Lord is your strength and stronghold.*
Nehemiah 8:10, AMP

But the fruit of the Spirit is love, joy, peace, longsuffering, gentleness, goodness, faith, meekness, temperance...
Galatians 5;22, KJV

Any normal school-day pressures and challenges can be an attempt at disrupting your peace and joy. Most people's interpretation of **joy** is happiness. Although joy can bring happiness, there is SO much more to it than that. In fact, if you study the word <u>joy</u> in the Strong's Concordance, you find that it means <u>calm delight</u> or <u>to be joined</u> (Strong's, entry #2302, 2304). The word **strength** is also interesting. It means, <u>a fortified place, a defense, a rock, or force</u> (Strong's 4581). The true spiritual force of JOY "joins" you to the power of God as you begin to allow it to rise up on the inside of you in any given situation. If you know Jesus as your Savior and have a living relationship with him, all of those things listed in the Galatians scripture are already on the inside of you because the Holy Spirit is on the inside of you. But it is up to you to make a conscious decision to operate in them.

When you walk in joy, you cannot walk in strife. When you give, joy is increased and developed. Nothing can keep you down if you keep the revelation of joy on the inside of you. Here is how NOT to lose your joy at the first sight of trouble:
1) **Start praising the Lord, even when you don't FEEL like it.**
2) **RUN to the Word and begin saying it out loud if necessary.**
3) **Laugh at adversity!**
4) **Give voice to joy. (Jeremiah 33:11)**

James 1:2 says, **"Count it all joy when you fall into diverse temptations."** One of my friends takes that seriously as she retreats to her prayer room and boldly proclaims, "Joy one, joy two, joy three, joy four…" God will meet those that rejoice, and when the force of joy rises up so strongly in you, troubles will look very small in comparison.

__Pray this prayer:__ Dear God, since the joy of the Lord is my strength, I will rise above adversity by praising and rejoicing even if and especially when I don't feel like doing so. I call upon what You put on the inside of me to carry me through any adversity. In Jesus' name, Amen.

What's On You?

Day 78

The Spirit of the Lord is upon me....
Luke 4:18, KJV

We do not dare to classify or compare ourselves with some who commend themselves. When they measure themselves by themselves and compare themselves with themselves, they are not wise.
2 Corinthians 10:12, NIV

As I began to be used more and more of the Lord to help put Bible as an elective into public schools, my activities became more diversified. Sometimes I spoke to school boards or community meetings; other times I participated in press conferences; often I just met with individual superintendents or school board members. But as time passed, I could see that the Lord was **"enlarging my coasts"** (1 Chronicles 4:10), and **"lengthening and strengthening my stakes"** (Isaiah 54:2).

Eventually an event presented itself that required me to participate in a television program with some very well-known people. Although I was very excited about doing it, and knew it would help to widely spread the news of our curriculum, I experienced some apprehension since I am definitely NOT well-known. I wrestled with nervousness for a few days beforehand, knowing anxiety is not of God. I knew God had called me to this, so I prayed and asked Him to give me light and wisdom on the whole situation. One night as I was reading my Bible before bed, He showed me that I must not ever compare myself to others. There could only be two outcomes and both would be in error. One outcome would be that I would feel INFERIOR, and the other would be that I would feel SUPERIOR. Then He showed me the scripture about the Spirit of the Lord being upon me. It "dawned" on me that the same Holy Spirit that is upon those well-known people is upon me as well. All I needed was to recognize and receive that, and lift my part, great or small, up to Him to multiply just as he did the loaves and fishes of the boy in the Bible. I also remembered that a few months before I had been not only praying, "The Spirit of the Lord is upon me," but also *singing* it! The television show went very well, and not only was I NOT nervous; I had a fabulous time with everyone!

Always, always trust God!

Prayer this prayer: *Dear God, the Spirit of the Lord is upon me. I lift up my portion to You. Multiply it and use it to bless others around me and to accomplish Your purposes. Help me to realize the futility in comparing myself to others. In Jesus' name, Amen.*

The Consequences of Complaining

Day 79

Do all things without complaining or arguing, so that you may become blameless and pure, children of God without fault in a crooked and depraved generation, in which you shine like stars in the universe as you hold out the word of life...

Philippians 2:24-26, NIV

One of life's most destructive forces is that of complaining or murmuring. It is has serious consequences, as we see in the book of Numbers. In the thirteenth chapter one member of each tribe, twelve total, were sent to search out the land of Canaan. They were to spy it out, gathering information about the strength of the people and about the land itself. They were also to bring back some of the fruit. On their return they reported that the land flowed with milk and honey. The one cluster of grapes they brought back required **two men** to carry it! The only problem was that there were giants in the land. All but two men, Caleb and Joshua (read your Bible and follow up on the successful lives of these two!), said the land couldn't be taken. In chapter fourteen it says, **"And all the children murmured against Moses..."** The consequences of that murmuring led to the children of Israel staying in the desert forty more years until a whole other generation had died!

Every day at school you have the opportunity to murmur and complain. I can remember several incidences when I had the opportunity to complain and the Lord cautioned me against it; there are no rewards for complaining. Perhaps there was the time you were coaching basketball and the head coach decided to have a tournament during the Thanksgiving holidays, leaving no time for rest or family. There may have been the time of the senior trip when you were assigned to ride the bus with the least well-behaved students. There may have been the occasion when you were sent to a staff development workshop in which you had absolutely no interest. Or perhaps you were asked to combine two different classes in the same class period.

Your choices involve either consequences or rewards. Refuse to be found murmuring or complaining and "shine like the stars in the universe, as you hold out the word of life."

Pray this prayer: *Dear God, help me to recognize opportunities to refuse to complain. Help me to see these times as times to shine. I choose not to be a complainer, but to do the best job possible and expect the rewards. In Jesus' name, Amen.*

Another Kind of Teacher

Day 80

Train up a child in the way he should go {and in keeping with his individual gift or bent} and when he is old he will not depart from it.

Proverbs 22:6, AMP

I would be remiss in the writing of this devotional book if I failed to honor another kind of teacher, the home school teacher. With public school problems escalating, more and more parents are choosing to educate their children at home. Many feel this to be the best way of instilling and maintaining solid traditional values.

Contrary to some of the misinformation about home schooled children, they tend to be well-educated and socially adjusted as well. My sister, Molly, home schools her four children. She amazes me at what she has been able to accomplish. In spending so much time with them, she recognizes their particular "bents" and directs their learning appropriately. My three nieces, Kelli, Sara, and Penny, and my nephew Jonathan, are far ahead of their pubic-schooled peers, especially in reading, vocabulary, and history. They excel in science and math as well. Kelli recently took her SAT and ACT exams for college entrance and scored so well that she was awarded a large scholarship at a local university. All four children are very active in gymnastics, baseball, dance, basketball and music. I would be hard-pressed to find any more well-adjusted, well-disciplined children anywhere. Also, they have had rigorous Biblical training that could not be available in public schools. It could be said that I am biased because of these children, but I also know many other families who home school their children. The story is the same.

I have watched my sister and brother-in-law and have seen the sacrifices they make for their educational choices. The results show it is well worth it. I applaud all parents that take on this monumental task. While public school is still playing the major role in the education of our children, having other options provides choices for parents who desire different structure and atmosphere for their own children.

Pray this prayer: *Dear God, thank You for home school teachers and their contribution to society. I ask You to bless them and the children they are educating. In Jesus' name, Amen.*

A Giving Mentality

Day 81

Give and it will be given to you; good measure, pressed down, shaken together, running over, they will pour into your lap. For by your standard of measure it will be measured to you in return.

Luke 6:38, NASB

And I will very gladly spend and be spent for you...

2 Corinthians 12:15, KJV

In our schools vacuums exist all around us that can be filled by giving our resources and spending ourselves. Many students come to us who are so needy in so many ways. Just about anything and everything we give to them fills a void. Teachers around us may be in need as well.

A line from a gospel song says, "Take whatever you have and give it away." What a different place the world would be if people everywhere had giving on their minds instead of taking. Our homes, schools, work places, and even churches suffer from a deficit of giving that stems from the absence of a "giving mentality". Generally this is due to a fear that "there won't be enough left over for me and my needs." Studying the spiritual law of giving and receiving proves that nothing could be farther from the truth. Each time one gives, a seed is planted that can only result in the harvest of much more. God, the greatest giver of all, set this example by giving His Son Jesus to die on the cross. The harvest is every man that chooses to trust and believe in His Son. What a harvest!

While giving may manifest in the form of money or material things, perhaps the highest way is giving of ourselves. Everywhere one goes one takes the supply of oneself, the greatest resource. Spending yourself in behalf of another human being takes on the nature of Jesus.

I encourage you to develop a "moment-to-moment" giving mentality. Always be on the lookout for a chance to meet a need or to bless another's life. These opportunities are always available; we just have to become sensitive to them. Expect to live the giving life at school, the grocery store, the beauty shop, the restaurant, the football game, church, and especially at home. Think ahead and plan on purpose to give. Never hesitate to part with something even on the spur of the moment if God tells you to give it to another person. Start right now and "take whatever you have and give it away." Walk in the love of God, give of yourself, and trust Him for your every need.

Pray this prayer: *Dear God, Teach me to be a constant giver. I want to follow Your example in giving. Make me aware of needs that I can fill. Show me about showing Your love through giving. In Jesus' name, Amen.*

His Way Is Always Success

Day 82

...a wise man's mind will know both when and what to do.

Ecclesiastes 8:5, AMP

    For three months we had been planning to attend a weekend women's conference. My two daughters-in-law and my stepdaughter had made arrangements far ahead to be off work to attend the conference that was my treat to them. The tickets had been purchased and all the arrangements made. My stepdaughter, Katherine, seemed particularly excited because it would be a much-needed break from her large class of very active fourth graders.

    On the Tuesday before the conference weekend, Katherine called to tell me that a field trip had been rescheduled, set to take place the very Friday we were all leaving for the conference. She was near tears. Because her principal had already promised her the time off, he was willing to remain faithful to that commitment. However, Katherine readily sensed that he needed her to go on the trip to assist in managing her class. She also knew that volunteer adults for the trip were scarce. We prayed together over the phone and she said she would let me know later as to her decision. The day before our conference trip, she emailed to say that she had prayed about it with her husband, and she strongly felt that she should attend the field trip. Although we all missed her presence at the conference, her own trip turned out very enjoyable, and Katherine knew she had done the right thing.

    Sometimes our choices may seem difficult, but if we will pray and commit our plans to Him, His way is always success. Be ready for divine interruptions. Perhaps you are today facing some difficult choices concerning requests made of you by your superiors. Take it to the Lord in prayer, and He will show you about His plans for success.

Pray this prayer: Dear God, I have some choices to make today. I want my choices to come into agreement with Your plans and purposes. Help me to hear Your voice clearly and to make successful choices. I roll my works upon You and commit them wholly to You. In Jesus' name, Amen.

A Time of Cleansing

Day 83

Search me, O god, and know my heart, test me and try my thoughts, see if I am taking a wrong course, and do thou lead me on the lines of life eternal.

Psalm 139:23,24, Moffatt's

At a conference recently, I heard a speaker say that statistics show that approximately 85% of young Christians walk away from their faith after the first year of college. It is also said that many universities promote classes with professors and teachings that encourage young people to question their faith. As a result, many of our young, new teachers are bringing more and more worldly, secular ideas to the classrooms. This is cause for concern because these ideas, coupled with other challenges facing our schools and students, provide opportunity to further reject our Godly heritage and the morals and values set forth by the Bible.

I encourage you to take an honest look introspectively and determine if your faith and Godly values are still intact. Did you attend a university that either overtly or covertly caused you to question your faith? Have you abandoned any solid Biblical teachings in favor of the secular humanistic and more widely accepted ideas that our society promotes? Have you been taught that public school is no place for God and Biblical values?

Our school children are desperately crying out for help, and sometimes a teacher is the only positive role model in their lives. We cannot fill their minds and hearts with any more worldly secularism than they're already soaking up from the media and other places. Psalm 51:10 says: **Create in me a clean heart, O God; and renew a right spirit within me.** If you answered "yes" to any of the above questions, you have been lied to, and it is time to cleanse your mind of these ideas and get back on the right track. Being led by the Spirit of God and operating in the mind of Christ (1 Corinthians 2:16) are your greatest assets in being a powerful, effective teacher. Saturate yourself in God's Word, and it will "penetrate even to the dividing of the soul and spirit" (Heb. 4:12). His light will reveal what needs cleansing.

Pray this prayer: *Dear God, I ask You to cleanse my mind and create in me a clean heart and renew a right spirit within me. I let go any secular humanistic ideas that are anywhere in my heart. Wash me clean with Your word and the blood of Jesus. Help me to pass on to my students only the ideas that are in agreement with Your Word. In Jesus' name, Amen.*

The Final Outcome

Day 84

I thank Christ Jesus our Lord, who has given me strength, that he considered me faithful, appointing me to his service.

1 Timothy 1:12, NIV

It was the beginning of August when my daughter-in-law, Sara, accepted her very first teaching job. The position was in an inner city school in the projects in a city in Texas. Although she had been out of college for a few years, she was working on her teacher certification and was thankful to have the job. Time was short, and my son and I pitched in to help her prepare her classroom for the challenging group of fifth graders soon to arrive. We cleaned, painted, and put up bulletin boards. We prayed over the classroom and every desk, and Sara herself. Little did Sara realize what lay in store.

The school year began, and I spoke with her often and prayed for her. I knew things were very difficult. Most of her students had no supportive home life. They were openly rebellious to the point of shocking her with their comments and actions. Sometimes the police were called in to school. Many times she called me with specific names to pray over. After one month she phoned me one day and said, "I just don't know if I can do this or not." I encouraged Sara to press into God's word and prayer, assuring her that He would strengthen her for this job if this was what He had called her to do. She did this, and one day she came to the final conclusion that she was indeed called to this position, and that **no matter what else happened, she was staying with it.** I believe that this was the turning point.

Sara began to truly fall in love with those children and to see them the way Jesus sees them. Although she experienced many other difficult situations, she never considered quitting again. She put her whole heart into teaching those students and just took one day at a time. By the end of the school year, not only did Sara have control over her classroom, and not only were her students showing considerable improvement, but she was also named an exemplary teacher and elected to attend a special conference for at-risk children.

If you are in a difficult teaching position today, do not lose heart. Turn to the Word of God and prayer, and draw on His strength and wisdom and **FINISH**.

Pray this prayer: Dear God, Sometimes I feel like quitting and running away. Help me to remember that You are right here with me because You said You would NEVER leave me or forsake me. Help me to love and see these children through Your eyes. I choose to stand strong in Your power and complete my appointment. In Jesus' name, Amen.

Two Job Descriptions

Day 85

The thief comes only in order that he may steal, and may kill and may destroy. I came that they may have and enjoy life, and have it in abundance—to the full, till it overflows.

John 10:10, AMP

Situated on the front lawn of our city's high school is a memorial with planted flowers and a stone sculpture of our mascot bulldog. The marker is a tribute to a beautiful young girl who actually played the role of the mascot that year on our team's pep squad. Her life prematurely ended in a car wreck. As additional counselors and pastoral staff arrived at school the next day, students lined up to seek answers to the nagging question of, "Why?"

I thank God for the Bible, which clearly outlines the job descriptions of both the devil and Jesus. In the book of John the words of Jesus leave no room for wonder. The devil is described as being here ONLY to steal, kill, and destroy. There is absolutely no life connected with the enemy, Satan. He detests us because we are made in God's image, and because we have access to the overcoming power of God so that we can walk in His plan and purposes and affect the lives of others here on the earth for Jesus. In direct contrast, JESUS came so that we could have and enjoy life! He came that we might have it in abundance (to the full, till it overflows!). Jesus died so that we could live.

So many people blame God for the bad things in their lives, forgetting that we have an enemy, the devil. This mostly comes from a lack of understanding of the nature of God. God only wants to do us good. He is a ***good*** God. Psalm 103:2-4 says, "**Bless the Lord, O my soul, and forget not ALL his benefits: Who forgiveth ALL thine iniquities; who healeth ALL thy diseases; Who redeemeth they life from destruction; who crowneth thee with lovingkindness and tender mercies."** Read on in that Psalm for other good news about the goodness of

God. The 91st Psalm speaks of the benefits of dwelling in the "secret place": deliverance from pestilence, terror, and evil plots; no evil befalling you; and being satisfied with LONG life. Stay with the Word and God even when you don't understand some things. Determine once and for all to never again confuse the job descriptions of the devil and Jesus. Let your Bible and the Holy Spirit help you keep them separate.

Pray this prayer: *Pray the 91st Psalm, inserting your name or another name in the appropriate places. Pray Psalm 103:1-6.*

My Favorite Teachers

Day 86

Shall they not teach thee and tell thee, and utter words out of their heart?

Job 8:10, KJV

I grew up in the sixties and seventies and have fond memories of being a student in the classroom. Though things were drastically changing around me, especially with the removal of prayer and Bible reading in the early sixties, I was not aware of it. I remember that era as a time when school was a very safe place.

When I think of certain teachers that made a mark on my life, I am reminded of the impact that I as a teacher may have on the life of another. My first grade teacher was a young woman, Miss Smith. At recess she played baseball with all of us on the dirt field in her dress and good shoes. She could really hit the ball and run the bases! Another teacher that stands out in my memory is my fifth grade teacher, Miss Steele. She was tough and seemed mean, but we all loved her. I still have the letters we wrote to one another during summer vacation that year. She answered every letter I sent to her. My parents divorced that year and it was comforting to have another adult that cared. My junior high band director, Mr. Dickason, better known as Mr. D, was retired from the military. He was TRULY tough and mean, but we had the best junior high band in the city at that time, and I learned a sense of discipline that shaped my actions and attitudes from that time forward. My high school journalism teacher, Mrs. Sparks, directed my desire to write. She was gently critical while encouraging me to continue the pursuit of putting my ideas and feelings on to paper.

These teachers and others imparted to me knowledge and wisdom, and they poured their hearts into all their students. We can say that school times were easier then, but that just serves to magnify the importance of being the teacher who makes a difference in this time. Even the smallest deposit into a student can make an indelible impression. Be aware and sensitive of opportunities all around you to impact your students in positive ways.

Pray this prayer: *Dear God, thank You for the wonderful teachers that You put into my own life. Thank You for the examples that they were and are. As that was sown into me, help me to sow into my students. I purpose not to miss any opportunities. In Jesus' name, Amen.*

Training For Eternity

Day 87

Exercise daily in God—no spiritual flabbiness, please! Workouts in the gymnasium are useful, but a disciplined life in God is far more so, making you fit both today and forever.
1 Timothy 4:7,8, The Message

Spend your time and energy in the exercise of keeping spiritually fit. Bodily exercise is all right, but spiritual exercise is much more important and is a tonic for all you do...
1 Timothy 4:7,8, TLB

While I was a high school teacher, I spent some time coaching girls' basketball. I was blessed to have a mentor coach who had coached state championship teams and was very knowledgeable about the game. Although I had played basketball in high school, this seasoned coach taught me much about new strategies and plays. I enjoyed the opportunity to get to know my students in a different setting. I also came into contact with the less positive side of coaching as I dealt with parents, some game losses, and overall criticism from different directions. I decided that a teacher's repertoire is seriously lacking if the coaching experience is absent!

We spent many hours in the gymnasium, the girls running plays over and over. We also incorporated many fundamental drills to sharpen their general basketball skills. The girls practiced teamwork strategies. Most of all we required them to do almost endless conditioning and weight training so they would be fit to go the distance and not tire or grow weary in a regular basketball game. All these elements work together to produce a winning team.

Spiritual fitness requires the same energy and dedication. I once heard a minister say that most people feed their bodies three hot meals a day and their spirits one cold snack a week. If this is true, how spiritually fit are we? Although being in great shape physically is a wonderful thing and necessary for our fleshly bodies, it will have no benefits in eternity. Daily Bible reading and study, prayer, and acting on the Word of God are what will keep us spiritually fit to be an effective warrior in the army of God. Doing these things on a regular basis, we will be prepared for the trials of life and will not tire easily, grow weary, or quit when the going gets tough. Take the "tonic" of daily spiritual exercise and be prepared for anything!

Pray this prayer: *Dear God, help me sharpen the skills of being spiritually fit. Help me to be a strong warrior in Your army. Holy Spirit, be my "sergeant," training me to grow stronger each day. In Jesus' name, Amen.*

By Faith

Day 88

Now faith is the assurance (the confirmation, the title-deed) of the things we hope for, being the proof of things we do not see and the conviction of their reality— faith perceiving as real fact what is not revealed to the senses.

Hebrews 11:1, AMP

The eleventh chapter of Hebrews is often called the Faith Hall of Fame. Each verse tells of great faith feats. Some of those mentioned involve Noah, Abraham, Jacob and of course, God. If possible, stop right now and read the entire eleventh chapter of Hebrews.

One of its verses says it is impossible to please God without faith. I was meditating on this and also on how faith plays a key role in walking out the teacher's calling. First of all it takes faith to even know your calling. It takes faith to day by day walk into a room full of students who think that you should know ALL the answers. It requires faith to believe that you can indeed impart knowledge to these given into your care for eight hours each day. On the most difficult days, faith is needed to stand firm and not waver from that place and calling.

The Bible says that God has dealt to every man the measure of faith (Romans 12:3). Despite this, many teachers may feel that their faith is weak or undeveloped. The good news is that this is easily remedied. Romans 10:17 says: **"Faith comes by hearing, and hearing by the Word of God."** As you hear, hear, hear the word of God, your faith will begin to grow. As you exercise it, faith will begin to produce more and more results. This is the way faith is developed and made strong. Our faith is NOT developed by trials and tribulations; if that were the case, we would all be faith giants! Trials and tribulations may drive us to TURN to the things that develop our faith (the Word, prayer, seeking God), but they in themselves are not faith builders. Finally, because it is confident, true faith RESTS.

Exercise your faith for the classroom by releasing faith-filled words. Here is a confession: **"I am strong in the Lord and the power of His might. In my classroom knowledge is imparted to open ears and hearts. I always have the right words for explanation. My students and I communicate clearly with each other. Apathy does not have a place in this room. Much learning takes place here."**

Pray this prayer: *Dear God, thank You for the measure of faith You have already given to me. As I read and study Your word, I allow it to grow me up in the area of faith. I will exercise my faith daily. In Jesus' name, Amen.*

Failure Sabotaged: My Story Part One

Day 89

Save me, O God, for the waters have come up to my neck. I sink in the miry depths, where there is no foothold. I have come into the deep waters; the floods engulf me.

Psalm 69:1,2, NIV

My teaching career began in the fall of 1984. I was almost twenty-nine years old. I had two young sons and had just gone through a divorce. My mind and emotions were spent. My only reason for entering the teaching profession was so that I could earn a salary and have as much time off as possible to be with my sons.

At the age of twelve I had walked the aisle of a church, had prayed the prayer of salvation, and had entered into water baptism that same night. But from there my life was a series of religious ups and downs, in church and out; I had no strong discipleship support system anywhere. By the time I reached college, I hadn't been to church in years, and I thought little about God. I finally did return to church; I even played the piano and taught Sunday school, but I had no personal relationship with Jesus Christ. Now here I was, with children to support and needing a support system myself. As a teacher, I went through the motions only; my sole thought was of the paycheck at the end of the month. I did not think or care whether I was a good teacher or a poor teacher; it was just a job. I would show up, put in my eight hours, go home and start all over again the next day. I knew things were not the best, and I looked for happiness and fulfillment in all but the right places. It never once occurred to me that God was my answer.

A few years passed, and I met and married my present husband. Although we were happy, I was very miserable in my teaching position. From my perspective, everything was wrong with the system and everyone else. It never once dawned on me that at least some of the problem might lie in my own heart. I didn't like the students, and I am certain they felt the same about me. I lived for Fridays, holidays, and summers. So many unpleasant events had happened during my teaching career that I believed myself to be an utter failure as a teacher. I knew something was missing. I resigned my job certain that another would quickly take its place. This did not happen. I felt so lost and undone. What now?

Pray this prayer: *Dear God, Purify me with hyssop, and I shall be clean. Wash me and I shall be whiter than snow (Ps. 51:7). Help me, Lord, for the waters have come up to my neck. Reach down, take hold of me, and draw me out of the deep waters (Ps. 18:16). In Jesus' name, Amen.*

Failure Sabotaged: My Story Part Two

Day 90

Then Jesus declared, I am the bread of life. He who comes to me will never go hungry, and he who believes in me will never be thirsty.

John 6:35, NIV

If the son therefore shall make you free, you shall be free indeed.

John 8:36, KJV

Shortly before I resigned my job, I was cleaning out a closet and came across a set of teaching tapes from a well-known ministry. My mother had given them to me sometime earlier. I suddenly had a strong desire to listen to them, and I played them as I drove back and forth to work. Little did I realize how the messages on those tapes would so change my life. When I did not get another job right away, I decided that I would use this time to study my Bible. In fact, I hoped never to enter the classroom again. So every morning for the **next two years** my routine was the same: I would take our children to school, come home and throw in a load of laundry, and plan for dinner. Then I would go to our bedroom, open my Bible, and play those tapes. Many times I stayed in that chair for six straight hours, or until I had to pick up my children and begin their activities. I acquired other tapes of sound, Biblical teaching. Slowly, ever so slowly, a transformation began. I fell in love with Jesus. I fell to my knees and rededicated my life to the Lord and asked him to show me His plan and purpose for me. During this time, many things began to change in our household as we all began to grow in God. We learned we could pray over everything from sickness in our bodies to college scholarship applications.

One day the high school principal called and asked if I would serve as a parent on a particular committee. I agreed.

After one of the meetings, he told me there was need of another Spanish teacher and asked if I would take the job. I froze in terror, remembering my hope to never enter the classroom again. I decided to discuss it with my husband. He was so gracious and told me whatever decision I made would be fine. But the very next morning at a women's prayer meeting, one of the women laid hands on me and prayed. She said that the Lord was calling me back into teaching, but this time as to a mission field. Despite the fear I felt, I knew God was definitely calling me. I also knew that for the past two years He had been preparing me. I took the position.

Day by day, God unfolded His plan. I spent the next several years in the classroom. I was a changed person from the one who had before been there. With fond memories of pleasant and exciting times, I now recall those years with students and other faculty. God used me to implement and teach the Bible elective at our school, and to later take that curriculum to many other schools. I was actually sad when I left the classroom to pursue that part of the plan full time. But oh! how exciting it is! That is what I continue to do today. God's faithfulness has been amazing as He continues to open doors for that opportunity in other school districts around this nation and even in some other countries.

God has a plan for you as a teacher. It will not elude you if you stay connected to Him. He wants you to know His will even more than you want to know it. Ask Him to make it plain to you and He will.

I leave with you the verses from Colossians chapter three that God gave to me when I re-entered the classroom: **Whatever may be your task, work at it heartily (from the soul), as something done for the Lord and not for men, knowing with all certainty that it is from the Lord and not from men that you will receive the inheritance which is your real reward. The One Whom you are actually serving is the Lord Christ, the Messiah. (v v. 23, 24, Amp).**

May God richly bless you and keep you as you continue on your journey as an educator in the army of the Lord.

Pray this prayer: *Dear God, thank You for clearly revealing Your plan and purpose to me. Make me acutely aware of the bigger picture. Teach me how to stay connected to Your Spirit moment to moment, that my every step is divinely directed of You. Give me discernment of the relationship purpose of each person You bring into my life, so that divinely ordained goals are met, and a lost and dying world is reached with the Gospel. In Jesus' name, Amen.*

Printed in the United States
136584LV00002B/3/A